What
The
Fuck!
LIFE OF A MEDIUM
Mark Hamilton

ISBN: 978-1-990330-04-9

Limits of Liability and Disclaimer of Warranty
The author and publisher shall not be liable for your misuse of the enclosed material. This book is strictly for informational and educational purposes only. The author and/or publisher do not guarantee that anyone following these techniques, suggestions, tips, ideas, or strategies will become successful. The author and/or publisher shall have neither liability nor responsibility to anyone with respect to any loss or damage caused, or alleged to be caused, directly or indirectly by the information contained in this book.

Medical Disclaimer
The medical or health information in this book is provided as an information resource only, and is not to be used or relied upon for any diagnostic or treatment purposes. This information is not intended to be patient education, does not create any patient-physician relationship, and should not be used as a substitute for professional diagnosis and treatment.

Editing, Layout and Design by One Thousand Trees
Printed in Canada by M&T Printing Group

Table of Contents

Acknowledgements

I want to thank three people for giving me the determination to be me, and for the work that I have done and the work to come. Thank you to Matt. He is a rock and pillar, and I really could not have done this without him. I have been allowed to be me, I and to do what I have needed to help people. I have also been given a lot of patience with the odd eye roll.

My grandfather—he stopped me many years ago from doing something that would have meant that I could not have done the wonderful and beautiful things that I have experienced in my life.

The last thank you goes to spirit- the divine- higher power - whatever label you wish to put on it. I thank you every day for giving me this gift, where there are no boundaries, walls or time. I have been blessed with meeting many people, sharing stories and experiences, and I have met some beautiful people. I am lucky but remember we are all born with this gift.

I also want to thank my dad who passed into the spirit world while I was writing this book. At least now you can see the work that I do with people. Some other spirit people that have helped me in my journey are Adam, Chris, William, Brock and Hutch and Lauren.

The reason for this book is a simple one. There are so many books out there that can help and educate, and so many life stories, but this needed to be a mixture, down to earth with the odd swear word to keep it real.

This book is a mixture of facts and stories and how I work. We all work differently so this isn't a book of criticizing others, and others' points of view; this is mine. I think the easiest thing with spirit is to get overloaded with being told to do this or that, and there is so much information out there. So one piece of advice I would give is: read, read, read, and then take on board any information that resonates. If it doesn't resonate, let it go. In my experience, the key to anything within spirit is trust. You will hear this a lot in the book. I write as I think, so there are bits that you really just have to read aloud in a British accent and remind yourself that spirit is fun as well.

Chapter 1

Me, Me, and a Bit More of Me

Hello all, my name is Mark and I talk to the dead. I actually prefer dead people over living folks, because I have found that dead people don't lie to me. I have been doing this for 9 years and have seen thousands of people. I do really enjoy my job But I don't like people. Strange you may say but all true. Spirit has always been around me and I didn't know it, but now I do. We are all born spiritual but as a child I didn't ever really hear of it until I started watching programs with John Edward and James Van Praagh.

I remember being in awe of what they would tell people, questioning where it came from and how they knew, but I never really connected the dots. I used to watch people and wonder, sometimes dreaming or thinking about their stories or what dead people there were, but I never gave it a second thought until much later. I later learnt that spirit is more visible to kids up to the age of 7, but it still didn't even ever occur to me that it could be me. I could be a medium. Me yes, fuck yes, me ...

I started this job by fluke. I had had some odd experiences as a child but I never really understood what it was all about. Spirit just started and in many ways I have never looked back but it's hard, emotionally. You kinda feel responsible on one hand about the messages you are giving, and then the emotions that the person sitting in front of you is dealing with. The more you work with spirit, however, this does change.

I love this job but I didn't start out this way. I was in social work and before that I worked in pubs and then homeless hostels and detoxes. All of this has helped me be the best I can be in my current job. I know that this will not be my last job, but I have not been told what's to come. It is a big part of the work, not necessarily being told what's to come from yourself and trusting that the universe will always provide what you need, even if you can't see it coming. If you would have said to me when I was 20 that I would be doing this, I would have laughed but I would change it now.

I started in 2012 and I have seen about 29,000 people and am currently booking about 5 years ahead. It's kinda crazy. In this work, you can turn it on and off but I don't. I love them and they keep me company, and working with spirit can be very lonely. I have found that many people just want me for what I can do and not for friendship. I get questions like, "Ooh can I just ask a question or 2?" or "Can you fit my friend in?" It is what it is. Working with spirit is lonely, because many people don't understand what I am seeing, feeling or hearing. Even though many people have their own experiences on a daily basis, they haven't understood that spirit is talking. Yes, you are not fucking crazy... I thought I was for a long time but the more I have worked, the easier it has become.

This is the thin line between a job I love and my human self that just at times . ok well a lot of the time ... wants to scream fuck off. But I will follow what I am told. Spirit has shown me that the world doesn't ever stop changing and that we as people don't either. I was asked a question recently about whether I remember the readings I do. The answer is no. I remember bits or snippets but not the whole thing. This is something I love because if I see people again, it's always a new experience.

I also say that I won't ask spirit stupid questions, which is why sometimes I will use the word I; that's me or them which is spirit.

In my time of working with the spirit world, there have been many stupid questions, some funny, others really out there, and some sad. The ones that make me sad are when people need validation that they are good enough, but I get that.

I have found that people do and will treat you differently, and there have been times when I have felt that I am a party trick. I recall being at a dinner party and the host asked me to say this and say this and impress them. I remember just standing up and leaving. I also recall a time when I was doing something at a lady's home and I could hear them talking about me. One lady was being very vocal as she viewed herself as perfect, and the others were not challenging her, and one person said, ``Well, he is just here for entertainment." I got up, walked out to the group and said I was leaving.

There was shock but afterwards I had some of them message me to apologize about that person and their behaviour, but once again they were not challenged.

Spirit work has taken time to grow. It's like dating the dead. You have to get to know each other's quirks, how you work, and how to interpret the images that you are given. Not all mediums work the same. I once heard some say I am a psychic medium. And others say a medium. I prefer to just say Mark. That's me... I am just me, I talk to the dead and I hear them.

When I first started working with spirit, I didn't understand the images and the thoughts and feelings I was getting. I used to see spirit more. I don't see as much now, but sometimes I hear, feel, see or just know. Other times it's a song, or I see a pair of eyes. They like to change things up and they don't like to warn you.

I work with a team of 3 guides and an angel. It's a collective and we work together. They help me see things and they guide me, but they don't tell me what to do. Everyone has them; some have more than others and sometimes you may not even know their names, but you learn how they feel. I will talk more of mine throughout the book and I may even show you a picture.

Every day with my work, I like to thank Spirit for what they do and how they help me. I feel that they have bettered me if that is the word. Spirit can help you as well, it's about asking for the help and being open to receive. Some people don't realize that just because you are spiritual, it won't always come easy, as spirit will give you what you can cope with. I have found that with reading, some people take a while to understand what I say. It can be frustrating and funny and at times hair pulling... I always bless them. Ok, maybe something else.

There have been times when I have been so confused about what the living are telling me, which is different to what spirit has told me but many times the people I'm seeing just don't get it or they are concentrating on areas of their life when I am talking about others. I would say that 99% of the time, they come back later and say that they now get it. It's hard not to take it personally but spirit teaches that trust is the key to working with them.

I want to say that I am not fearful of death and the process, because I know where I will end up. Heaven is a place of peace, joy, happiness and learning, and I always tell people that your spirit people don't miss you as they are all around you, but you miss them as you can't connect to them in the same way as you once did.

As I was writing this book, so many thoughts crossed my mind about where I am supposed to be. What am I supposed to be doing? Who am I supposed to be helping? Why do I get so frustrated with people and organizations in this world? What is next?

The answer is I don't know, and that's okay. I am human and to be human I have to experience all these things to become the best version of myself. I look around and often think what the fuck but I just have to smile and move forward. In a strange way, it took the death of my dad to accept some of these things.

Dad, I love you. I posted on my page about the loss of my dad and so many beautiful people wrote so many beautiful things. It reminds me of my human side, and I forget this at times. It's not that I forget that I am human, it's just that although I can connect to the spirit world I go through these human experiences on a daily basis . and this is the life I have chosen.

Next time you think Why me? Why did this happen? What did I do wrong? ... the answer is you are human but you also chose your experiences before you came into your present body. Don't forget who you are, and how wonderful you are. We are all learning, and works in progress.

Chapter 2

What is a Medium, Really?

There is a lot of confusion about what a medium is, and does. A medium is a third-party element through which two or more parties communicate; in other words, a medium is someone who can connect with the spirits on the other side.

As an indistinguishable and unavoidable part of human life, for intellectuals, artists, and even for common people, death has always been a place of meditation, imagination, and hope. To see a person's history, current and future events by tapping into the mystical energies around the person, a medium utilizes his or her psychic or intuitive ability. Some people think and believe it's mind reading. It's really not.

This means that, to gain the knowledge important to the individual being read, the medium depends on the existence of non-physical energy outside of themselves.

The very questions about the essence of death and what remains after death have been raised by religions, beliefs, and customs in many ways and shapes, and for many millennia. In the death-related rituals and traditional actions, from the periods close to one's death before the funeral, burial, and remembrance services, these questions influenced attitudes concerning the idea and experience of death, and these attitudes have been expressed and symbolized.

Mediumship

Mediumship is the process of mediating contact between deceased souls and people that are alive. People who practise it are called "mediums" or "spirit mediums" or in my case just Mark. There are numerous ways of mediumship or supernatural channeling, including tables of seance, table tipping, trance mediumship, and Ouija.

During the 19th century, when people used Ouija boards as a means of recreation for the upper classes, mediumship gained prominence. Over this time, inquiries uncovered systematic fraud, with some practitioners using tactics used by stage magicians, and the profession started to lose its good reputation.

In the medium/psychic market, fraud is already rife, with reports of deceit and trickery being uncovered to this day. The best gift of knowledge I can give you regarding fake mediums is to trust yourself. I don't believe a medium should be asking for more money. If the price has been paid, it's been paid. There could be further services that you agree on, but this should not be a pressured thing. Also I don't believe that a medium or psychic can guarantee that, if they perform a healing or a ceremony, you won't get sick, you will marry the person you want, etc. If that happens I would walk. We will talk later about what makes a good reading, when to go for a reading, and not relying on mediums for all answers.

In spite of the lack of reliable evidence for its existence, confidence in psychic ability is common. Scientific scholars have tried to ascertain the authenticity of mediumship statements.

There are many distinct mediumship types; arguably the best-known types include a spirit supposedly taking hold of the voice of a medium and using it to give a message, or where the medium actually 'hears' and passes on the message. Other types include materialization and telekinetic operation of the spirit, or the appearance of a voice.

History of Mediums and Mediumship

Back in early human history, attempts to interact with the deceased and other living humans, aka ghosts, were noted. The tale of the Witch of Endor ('witch' is made 'medium' in the passage) in the most current translation of the NIV of the Bible, talks of one who lifted the soul of the fallen prophet Samuel to encourage the Hebrew king Saul to question his previous tutor about a fight to come, as reported in the Books of Samuel in the Jewish Tanakhah (the basis of the Old Testament).

Mediumship in the United States and the United Kingdom in the 19th century became very prominent with the advent of Spiritualism as a religious revolution. Early Spiritualism in New York State is also said to stem from the Fox sisters' rituals and tutorials in 1848. The more you read about the past and where it started the more sense it makes. In the mid-19th century, Paschal Beverly Randolph and Emma Hardinge Britten were two of the most renowned instructors and writers on the subject. The word Spiritism was invented by Allan Kardec around 1860. Kardec indicated that the foundation of his *The Spirits' Book* and later, his five-book series, *Spiritist Codification,* was experienced with souls by chosen mediums.

Many scholars also became converts of the time, and practised spiritualism. The chemist Robert Hare, the scientist William Crookes (1832-1919) and the evolutionary biologist Alfred Russel Wallace (1823-1913) showed their concern and interest. In the work of Eusapia Palladino, the Nobel laureate Pierre Curie developed a rather serious scientific role. Other notable members included William T. Stead (1849-1912), a writer and pacifist, and Arthur Conan Doyle, a doctor and poet (1859-1930).

Mediumship has come into disrepute in response to physical mediums such as the Davenport Brothers, as well as the Bangs Sisters, and the fraudulent use of theatre magic tricks. Nevertheless, faith and its values remain amidst this, with physical mediumship and séances arising from reality, and mediumship rising to the surface on the web.

In addition to vibrant microcultures of platform mediumship and 'home circles' in the late 1920s and early 1930s, there were about one quarter of a million active Spiritualists and about two thousand Spiritualist organizations in the UK. In the United Kingdom, Australia, Canada and the United States, Spiritualism tends to be practised mainly by numerous denominational Spiritualist denominations. Remember that mediums can be religious as well. I really believe that we all actually believe in the same things but sometimes have different names for them.

Clairaudience

Clairaudience is, simply, "clear hearing," or the ability to perceive other dimensional sounds and voices, usually from dead spirits at séances. Many clairvoyants are also clairaudient. A spiritualistic medium may accept messages from spirits in different ways. The medium may "hear" what the spirits say inside their head, or may see and describe the actions of spirits, almost like in a game of charades. The medium may also simply sense what is being passed on. Although there are others, these are the predominant types of clairaudient activity.

Hearing what is conveyed is almost like hearing someone whispering in your ear, although no one else physically present can detect the sound. It may also be close to sensing, except that in your ears, you sense the speaker and the words themselves, but are not sure of the actual sound that originates. Clairaudience may also contain poetry, lyrics, and other sounds that are heard.

I see spirit this way most of the time, and although it's unnerving to hear random thoughts or words, it's also very cool.

Clairaudience can also be encountered right before you fall asleep, or just as you are waking in the hypnagogic and hypnopompic states. It can also occur during meditation. The case of Joan of Arc was a classic example of clairaudience. In the fifteenth century, she heard voices that she credited to heaven and separate angels. At the age of thirteen, in her father's backyard, she first heard a sound that she claimed originated from heaven. She heard voices two to three days a week over the next five years, and was able to differentiate them from Saints Catherine, Margaret and Michael. To return the Dauphin to his throne, her voice led her to lead the French army against the English.

Other examples include Samuel, Moses, Solomon, and other Bible characters who thought they had heard God talking. In the same way, daimons or genii, considered as guardian spirits, heard muttered suggestions from the ancient Greeks. Socrates believed to have been instructed by a certain daimon. In the eighteenth century, the English poet William Cowper was informed of future events in his life by voices he heard in his ear. Wolfgang Mozart heard music in his mind and merely wrote down, note for note, what he had heard. In the late 1920s, Aura May Hollen started writing her many poetry books and songs from what had been assigned to her in her head. People have been guided throughout history by voices they have heard either internally or externally.

Clairaudience is often mistaken for "direct voice," which is very different in reality. Direct speech happens when, using the medium's vocal cords, the medium communicates in the voice of a dead spirit or, more specifically, a spirit speaks through the medium.

Seashells can also be used initiate clairaudience. Keeping a seashell to the ear and listening will eventually lead the listener, possibly momentarily blurry and far-off, to discern human voices. These voices get louder and clearer over a period of time, before distinct speech is heard, and even human voices are understood. I know many people that have huge issues with constant ear ringing. As a production instrument, a disconnected telephone may also be used.

The purpose is also fulfilled by an imaginary telephone. The medium picks up or imagines carrying the receiver and can hear a voice at the end of the line. Many mediums do this as a means of "turning on" the gift of clairaudience. They're going to picture a phone behind them and they're going to know that when it rings (in their head), there's going to be a ghost waiting to talk to them. I have had people ask whether they can talk to Elvis or Princess Diana. The answer for me is NO. It can be so fucked at times as people believe that it is a phone and they can talk to anyone, but, alas, it's not true.

Clairsentience

Clairsentience literally means "clear feeling"—the desire to sense energy clearly. It is not a strange, odd, spooky or paranormal 6th sense reserved for the 'special few' in comparison to the current common belief and modern day dictionary definition, but rather a naturally inherent and spiritual faculty that lives within us all.

We are each born all-knowing, and with the capacity to distinctly sense what is of the divine love that we are made of and what is not, because our heart is love. That is, we have an absolute understanding of the quality of energy that pulsates from within our inner heart, and so we know when this love is accompanied by every feeling, expression or deed, and when it is not.

Our five senses (sight, taste, touch, smell, sound) allow us to collect knowledge about our physical surroundings at a solely temporal level, and our 6th sense allows us to distinguish the energy field at play within it. All is energy, after all, so it makes sense for us to have a means by which to experience this. We have had the sense of going into a room and instinctively wondering whether everything is 'right,' even though everything on the surface appears good. This is because, even before our other organs perceive it, our heart knows everything.

Naturally, when we are children, we make our way through life through this sense rather than any other, sensing with our entire spirit, through our bodies, with our being. It's something we're not taught to do, but it happens naturally. Inherently, we understand which adults are safe to be around and which are not. We do not doubt this ability until we begin to understand that this sense is not used by the majority of people in the country. In reality they appear to be totally missing it.

Therefore, because the universe is not actually set up to deal with, let alone help, this inherent faculty to thrive, we learn to shut it down much of the time. It can never be fully shut down, in fact, but we learn that by not using it, we are compensated and thus learn to adhere to a way of life that has us voicing even less than our true self.

I have many experiences of this on a daily basis, and I know through mentoring that a lot of my students have experienced this as well. It's a battle to work out who it is, what is being said, and to whom the message needs to be given. It goes back to my favourite word: trust.

Basically, in the first five or so years of life, we learn to feel the degree to which people around us live according to their essence, and whether we would be welcomed if we live true to ours. Then we are told to believe only what we see from our eyes and to override the signs from our inner heart, the place where our real self, our spirit, resides. In this way, instead of living according to the nature (the wisdom of God/the Universe) that we sense within us, we cause ourselves to be fed by the outside realm of values, ideologies and images. This is because we have come to champion emotions, and identifying with what we do rather than who we are. We continue to establish habits from this early age that help us fit in with others around us, even though they do not live according to who they are.

It is a bit like walking around in the dark while carrying a flashlight that can lead you, but you don't turn it on because no one else has turned on their flashlight. You wonder whether it should be turned on, and if you manage to work your way through all this and eventually turn it on, you have already calculated the degree to which you will stick out. You know that all eyes will be on you, so you keep the dimmer switch close so that you can calibrate the light according to the impact it has in terms of how comfortable/insecure it makes everyone else feel.

Clairvoyance

Clairvoyance (from French clair meaning "clear" and voyance meaning "vision") is the alleged ability to gain information about an object, individual, place, or physical phenomenon through extrasensory perception. Any person alleged to have such ability is then claimed to be a clairvoyant ("one who sees clearly").

The nature of spiritual and psychic powers, such as clairvoyance, has not been verified by modern research. This hypothesis is tested by parapsychology, but the scientific world does not understand the existence of the paranormal.

How Mediums Help Interact With Other Spirits

There are many ways in which mediums can facilitate "conversations" with the deceased. Some choose to undertake possession, serving as a vessel to communicate with this environment for any souls who require a physical figure. Some mediums are also empathic and are also likely to be able to communicate the views of people on both sides of the world. They can connect as clearly with ghosts as they can with those in this earthly world. There are plenty of us dancing in dimensions perpetually. I like to say that I spend more time in the spiritual realm than the living realm. I prefer it.

Mental Mediumship

Mental mediumship is the telepathic connection of souls with a medium. The medium hears (clairaudience) mentally, sees (clairvoyance), and experiences (clairsentience) spirit signals. The medium transmits the information to the recipient(s) of the message, either directly or with the aid of a spirit guide. When a medium is "reading" for a specific individual, that individual is known as the "sitter."

Trance Mediumship

Trance mediumship is also used as a type of mental mediumship. During a communicating phase, most trance mediums remain awake, during which time a spirit uses the mind of the medium to interact. The spirit or spirits using the mind of the medium influence(s) the mind with the feelings being communicated. The medium requires the ego to step back to transmit the message. Around the same time, with one's own bias, one has knowledge of the emotions flowing in, and can also affect the message. As the habits are totally different, such a trance is not to be mistaken with sleepwalking.

The action of extreme concentration of consciousness, which is the primary psychological process of trance induction, results in trance phenomena. Adaptive reactions in the brain are 'tuned' into neuronal networks, like institutionalized modes of trance.

There were very popular trance mediums in the 1860s and 1870s. In general, spiritualism drew female followers, many of whom had clear social justice ambitions. On abolitionism, temperance, and women's suffrage, many trance mediums gave passionate speeches. Leonora Piper has been described by scholars as one of the most popular trance mediums in the history of Spiritualism.

I have watched a wonderful lady in the UK do this and it's mind blowing. She allowed her whole self to step aside to allow the spirits of three people to flow through her. The demonstration lasted about 90 minutes and she spoke in different voices, mannerisms and content. I am not sure that I am ready for this yet but it's so cool to watch another do it.

I have allowed in deep meditation my soul or spirit to step aside and allowed spirit to flow with so much peaceful joy. No words were spoken but I was just a pure vessel, in the moment. I do this in a different way when channeling.

Physical Mediumship

The medium does not have a good memory of all the signals received in the traditional deep trance while in an unconscious state; these individuals typically work with a helper. The individual systematically writes down or otherwise records the voice of the medium. The assistant seldom mentions the sitter and other attendants' answering circumstances. An instance of this sort of partnership can be seen in the cooperation between Mrs. Cecil M. Cook of the Chicago William T. Stead Memorial Center (a particular religion existing under the laws of the state of Illinois) and the writer Lloyd Kenyon Jones at the turn of the 20th century.

Physical mediumship is described as the manipulation of the divine force and power system. Tangible appearances, such as noisy raps and sounds, voices, existing objects, contributions, eventuated spirit beings, or parts of the body such as hands, legs and feet, are thought to entail this form of mediumship. For such spirit embodiments, the medium is used as an energy source. This was achieved using the released energy or ectoplasm of a medium. The final physical medium to be studied by a scientific American committee was Mina Crandon in 1924.

The majority of physical mediumship is performed in a darkened or dimly lit space. A typical collection of instruments and appliances, including levitation tables, spirit cabinets and spirit trumpets, is used for most physical mediumships.

Difference Between a Medium and a Psychic

There is a big distinction between the two. Not all psychics are mediums but all mediums are psychics. What this means is that the psychic is basically at the entry level and the medium is taking it to the next level. It is a much more involved process, and it is almost a specialty of psychic ability. So, psychics are basically tuning in to the energy field of the person they are reading, and they are picking up on information about their past, present, and future, while mediums are relying on outside energies, and discarnate beings. So, your departed loved one's angels and spirit guides feed them the information so that they can carry on a conversation between two worlds.

A medium is a psychic who has disciplined whose extra-sensory experience and may speak to the realm of the soul. This literally means that a medium will send you guidance from other sources and powers, and then go to the realm of the soul to connect with loved ones, guides of the spirit, and the spiritual, to deliver you a full message.

Both are precious; it all depends on what kind of reading you prefer. Some people offer a psychic reading of the intuitive. Intuitive means the Divine's voice (guides, God, angels), whereas psychic means contact between soul and soul.

Why is a Medium Different from a Clairvoyant or Psychic?

It can be confusing to differentiate between mediums, psychics and clairvoyants. Many believe the words are synonymous, but that is not the case. Mediums are able to raise their vibration high enough to connect to the other side; psychics have the ability to provide information about the past, the present, or even the future, but not to deliver messages from the other side; whereas "clairs" usually interpret better messages, i.e., clairvoyants see clearly, clairaudients hear clearly, and clairsentients feel clearly.

These people "usually see time and space." It is important to remember, though, that one ability is not better than the other. All serve a purpose. Clients should hope to "hear from" dead relatives and/or loved ones because mediums supposedly engage with people who have passed on. The details of your sitting can vary, however each medium works in different ways. You have to be open to an intuitive experience, as well as receive messages that you may not have asked for. Expect some form of guidance, perspective, clarity, and authenticity." Mediums are individuals who occupy a heavy gap so that they are not kept to an unequal level. I think people will always get confused about this because they just don't understand. I am known as a psychic medium because I talk about future events, but as I have said all the information I receive is from the spirit world. I prefer the name Mark.

Throughout the centuries, these concepts, imaginations, habits, and practices and, in short, these actions, have shaped their own past. Two ancient and large cultures with their own distinctive characteristics and attitudes towards existential subjects such as mortality are the Western and Persian civilizations. The speech of the "Western attitude" has been argued to involve a kind of overgeneralization and misunderstanding of the diversity that occurs within Western cultures.

However, as seen in Philippe Aries' seminal work, general cultural patterns and mentalities in Western society can be found with a clear approach and defensible outcomes. In Western civilization and in Christianity, pagan schools of thought, enlightenment, and modernity, thoughts and attitudes toward death were under the influence of their Greek/Latin roots. However, the Persian attitudes were under the influence of Zoroastrianism, Islam and its Shi'a denomination, Sufism, and modernity (the old Persian religion that was the official religion of the Sassanid Empire before the Islamic period). In the literary wisdom of Persia, the gist of these attitudes was presented.

The Persian poetic wisdom is a vast body of Persian poetry that bears the collective knowledge and shared historical memories of Persian-speaking people, with a special role across centuries in transmitting culture and morality.

I have been asked what makes a good reading... Well there are many opinions and thoughts on this. I have a few of my own. I feel that a good reading has to feel connected, like you are understanding where the reader is coming from, that they are telling you things that you can connect to and they are not so general that it could connect to anyone.

The information that is being shared can be about living people and current information, but it can also connect to people that have passed. It depends on the type of reading you are going for.

Personally, I like to be challenged. I also feel that you should be able to record your own session. I have been to both types of readings, and I recall a few saying that I couldn't record due to the fact it stops a spirit connection. I'm not sure that I believe that.

I was once told that I was leaving my partner for a big black man and he wanted all my money. I remember laughing at this because, alas I don't have any money, but I did share this with the reader and my partner. It hasn't happened up to now.

Readings can also be subject to interpretation . I personally like detail, and prefer the reader to be consistent and not keep changing their story when I haven't connected to information. I think you also have to remember that some readers talk about future stuff so you have to be open. If you are unaware of something, just file it in the filing cabinet in your mind. I know that there are many clients of mine that I have told stuff to, and they didn't understand at the time, but found out the meaning later.

The last thing is about being open to what you receive. If you don't feel like they are connecting within the first 10-15 minutes, let them know. The key is going with an open mind, open heart and open spirit, and being prepared to be shown how people see you. This is not only difficult but in many ways painful.

I have had experiences in readings that I have given when the person didn't want to hear the truth. Their expectation was to feed into how they saw things. In most of these cases I found out later from others that truth was spoken but they just didn't want to see it.

As a reader the most important thing that I have seen and accepted is that truth always comes out. I have talked about affairs, murders, missing people, deaths coming up, and about love and life, but I don't predict death.

Chapter 3

My Journey Within the Spirit World

Learning to love myself is a journey that I am still working through. Just because I can smile when I need to doesn't mean that I am actually happy. There have been days when I have felt unworthy, unloved and unwanted, but I have had many days in which I have felt loved and needed. BUT the key is finding that within you as no one can find it for you.

What's your balance? I don't personally believe that I, or anyone, can be ecstatic at all times and that is honestly ok... I have had times in my life where I have felt enough is enough and, in looking back, that has happened when others have made me feel that way, whether it was friends or family or people in the same industry in which I work. Loving myself is a process, and it's not an easy one. Every day I have people saying thank you for this or that, or expressing how grateful they are for something that spirit has said to them. It's funny because I hear it, BUT I don't HEAR IT. I think a lot of people have the same issue.

Every day I listen to several songs that remind me where I am in my life; songs that give me strength and power to be the best person I can be. I can sing along and no one knows. My singing isn't a talent that I would say needs to be supported... To be honest, it would cause pain to those that listen to it.

I also have a mantra that I tell myself daily. I will share it with you because I can. I say. "I am loved, I am honoured and enough". I also look at my two tattoos which represent the words I am enough, and I thank the spirit for everything that I have in my life, both that which is good and not so good, because it's all the lessons that I need to see, feel, and hear. Some days I say FUCK IT, others I say why, but in reality these are all the things that I need in order to be the best version of myself.

This is a hard one as I learned the hard way... Spirit is energy and people take it out of us, whether it through advice, drama, or just needing something. It took me a while to get it, and I ended up in the emergency room as I thought I was having a heart attack. I was waiting for tests in the waiting room and my phone rang- I answered and someone was asking to book an appointment. I was on the phone for 45 minutes before I got my aha moment. The lady asked me to book an appointment. I was explaining repeatedly where I was, but she kept asking when I would be home. I explained again and she didn't understand. The lady asked me what time I would be home. The lightbulb went on. I said that I didn't think I was the right person for her. I put the phone down and I changed there and then.

One last thing was when I was at a party with a patron. While at the party she was very receptive to what was being told; she was agreeing, and giving examples, and then she told the host how much she enjoyed it. Later, she emailed me and told me that she thought it was a little too expensive and not everyone got the same length in messages. She said that she was disappointed for them, that she could do a better job, and that I should reduce my fees. I did tell the host and then later I cancelled another party at the same place when I found out this person was coming again... I refuse to waste spirit's and my time, and no one would challenge her about her behaviour.

Mediumship to me means many things. I am not a religious man, but I have faith in what I am being shown on a daily basis. However, I don't believe that religion and spirituality can go hand in hand together. I have seen clips of the heavenly realm and I do believe that we all go to heaven. I don't have the belief in hell as I feel we have already been in hell with some of the lessons in our current lives, that we experience through deaths, work, friendships, or just ordinary life experiences. As a medium , I am just me. I don't understand what happens, I don't understand how I do what I do, it just happens. BUT what I do believe is that we are all born with this "thing" that we do, but it's others that change our perceptions of what we believe and disbelieve. This is actually such an important reminder that we are all the same.

For me, mediumship and mediums vary greatly from person to person. I haven't yet met anyone like me, partly because I use the Fuck word a lot, but also because I am very honest and I don't just want to humour people. I feel that if I am not honest, or I lie to someone to allow them to hear what they want, it's not helping them at all.

I believe that the honesty and integrity I display in what I do has helped me a great deal in dealing with other mediums. I have seen many mediums that are awful, and others that are awesome. I have been told things like "My wife is amazing etc," "My house is...," "My kids are ..." and they haven't resonated at all, but then other people have told me stuff that I think HOLY FUCK. Yes, it does still shock me. If something is not connecting, I always tell the medium as there is no point wasting time, BUT I also put many walls up around me to block people. I know that's not good, but I drop the walls when I know that the information is connecting. There are things that I won't connect until later, so I will never say NO NO NO NO NO; I will say I'll think about it.

I have met many people in my travels within the spiritual realm. Some have been great, and others have been a lesson for me. This is something that is hard to learn, but necessary. I have worked with others but now I am on my own as I had been warned by spirit but didn't listen, and then it bit me in the arse. On my own I am in control of what I do and don't do. It's like we all have the lessons to learn but we should never be taken advantage of by others. It's hard to hear people telling lies or stories about you but in a sense it's flattery, and it's a chance to refuse to take others' emotional baggage on. This is a part of the soul contracts that we make before we arrive in this incarnation. Just because you start with someone, it doesn't mean that you have to end with them. That holds true for both family and friends.

My spirit team, such as my angels and guides, are always there to help and support you, but it's about finding and making a working relationship with them. It's like meeting new friends and finding how you work together. You just have to ask them for help.

They are not there to do it for you, but they will guide and support you in this journey. They help you learn all the lessons that need to be learnt in life before it's your time to go back to source. We always have free will in what we do, but the same doors will continue to be pushed at us until we experience all that is meant. All spirit guides have been human at one time, so they do understand the highs and lows of the living.

Chapter 4

Ego and the Highs and Lows

Ego: "a person's sense of self-esteem or self-importance"

Everyone has ego, and although it's not a bad thing, you will have to recognize that the ego and the spirit are very different, and you have to remove one to allow the other to flow.

Forgiveness is a powerful way to let go of ego; it will allow new doorways to your soul and remove your own blocks and negativity. Honesty is powerful as well. Learn to look at what you have in your life, both good and bad, and figure out what you no longer need to carry. You have probably heard the saying, "Silence is golden." I would say that there are no truer words.

Self-care

We as mediums can sometimes get confused as to our actual role. We have to be careful about walking the thin line between enabling, and helping and supporting. We can't do the work for someone but we can show people how to do it for themselves.

To enable someone can actually disempower them, as we all have to learn our own lessons. If we continually enable and don't allow natural consequences or order, the same lessons will repeat and we will become stuck in a cycle. I also believe that some people like the concept of free will, while others don't want to move forward due to fear and laziness.

In many conversations that I have had, some people have said that they believe they have to rescue their family or friends, but spirit (from my experience) and I do not agree. I believe that people have to learn lessons, and if they don't or they are not allowed to, they will continue to repeat the life lessons, and not necessarily in this current incarnation.

You will see later, when I talk about past life regression. An example could be someone who has mental health issues. They need to find their help, find the route of their own issue. You can't help them, but you can support them. You can be with them, help find people that could help, and be an emotional support in accessing the help.

I once saw a lady talking over someone. I have been guilty of this at times too, you have to allow the person who is needing the support to share their words and not yours when supporting someone

I was talking to someone about using the word NO more, and they said that NO is a bad word.- But for me, NO means owning my own choices, and becoming empowered because of it. Also remember we can't be victims in our own decisions. I had once talked to a lady that was attacked, and while talking through the trauma with her, the word no for her was so powerful. She was a survivor. She said that she chose to be a survivor.

I have the right to say no to people. I am still working through that one, and it has been key to my own mental health and wellbeing. I can't be there for people 24 hours a day. Nor can I respond to the 1300 emails and messages I receive in a month. It has taken me a long time to get to the point where I do not respond at 2 or 3 am because I don't want to disappoint. I have had people message me 10 minutes after their initial email, asking for a reply as I hadn't replied yet.

I have to own this. Others have pointed out that I was the cause because I kept on doing it. I am learning this lesson. It's not easy and I still fall into this trap. But I own it.

I have learnt that I have to be comfortable in saying no. I have to accept that I am important and that life is so short, and that I have a right to be me and do what I need for me. Remember you have this simple right as well. It's time for you to fly. Always remember that you are not wrong for putting yourself first.

When you say no to someone it can be a scary thing, as many thoughts of disappointment or heartache, and the thought of letting that person down, can overwhelm you. But if you think about it, you are empowering yourself. You are taking control.

It's time to think about a time where you said yes but should've said no. How did you feel? How much did the feeling weigh you down? If you had said no, what would have been the worst thing that could have happened?

Spiritual cleanliness is something that I try to live by. It's always a work in progress, and it's something that I have to self-check on a daily basis. These words mean clean soul, clean mind, clean actions, and finally staying emotionally clean.

As humans, we all make mistakes, but we have to forgive ourselves as each mistake is a learning lesson. Just remind yourself why you made that decision before you realized it was a mistake. You can't go back, but you can own and move forward so it doesn't happen again.

The dreaded overthinking and over-analyzing is something many people suffer with. There isn't an easy fix; it involves time, meditation or deep breathing, and constantly re-evaluating the important things in your life. And the most important thing: How far have you moved forward?.

Are you able to look into the mirror and see what others see? This is such an important step, and it's this that will provide you with a clean soul. Are you someone with integrity, honesty and respect? Remember this mirror will show you all your imperfections, so you have to be ready for it.

When you choose to take on energy and drama that is not yours, you will feel it. Your health will be affected and you can feel so heavy. To be spiritual, or even to be the best version of yourself, the best thing that you can do is recognize what's yours and what's not.

The feeling of sadness or happiness out of nowhere, regret or anxiety when you are around certain people, or the feeling of being so up and down without knowing where it stems from can actually be others' emotions that you are taking on. Once you recognize that these are not yours, it's time to let them go.

One way to help yourself is to ask to ground and bubble yourself, protect yourself, and ask your spirit to help you feel only what you need to, and let go of anything that doesn't serve you. I do this while in the shower every morning. I visualize tree roots coming from my feet and going into mother earth . I also ask to surround myself with white light, and only ask to feel my stuff. I have found that, when I feel something I'm not sure of, I will often say to spirit, "If this is not mine, please remove it." It works, but if you are feeling stuff and are not doing anything to let it go or work through it, it will remain. It has become your choice to keep it.

Grounding and bubbling can really change the way to feel quite quickly, but it is something that has to be done on a daily basis and sometimes multiple times a day depending on where you are. Some people have likened it to feeling a peace that they can't quite put their finger on.

Doing this means that you can start the process of working on you and not being overwhelmed by everyone who surrounds you.

I find myself burning incense on a daily basis, warding off others' negative energy and focusing on what's mine and what's not. I think that the majority of people walk around without realizing or understanding what they are feeling, and more importantly whose feelings they actually are.

Over my years of working with people it's become so important to check in; to check my internal body temperature in a spiritual sense, as empaths will always feel things that become overwhelming.

Crystals are something that I love using. I have them in my home, my workspace, my pockets, and I often give them to people.

Some of my favourites:

Selenite - Cleanses negative energies. Helps with receiving guidance and contacting spirit guides.

Amethyst - Known for its healing powers and ability to calm the mind.

Citrine - Releases negative traits, depression, fears and phobias. Emotionally balancing, energizing and recharging.

Tiger's Eye - Balanced energies and polarities, affirmed boundaries. Enhances clairsentience.

Black Tourmaline - Amplified protection for you and your space.

Fluorite - Heightened intuition. Clears confusion and improves decision making.

Rose Quartz - Opens the heart and increases the ability to love oneself and others.

Smoky Quartz - Brings emotional calmness, relieving stress and anxiety. Promotes positive thoughts and action.

These are some of many out there. I personally don't believe that bigger crystals are necessarily better. If in doubt go with your own intuition and gut when picking the right ones for you. It's also known that children are the best at picking crystals because they have the purity to go with what's needed at the right time.

It is best to cleanse crystals after purchasing, but please remember that not all crystals are good with water.

Smudging and cleansing is also needed, in whatever way works for you.

Chapter 5

Spiritual Practice

Developing Your Spiritual Practice

It can be just as necessary to cultivate and grow your spirituality as eating a balanced diet, exercising, and developing good relationships. It will strengthen your sense of relationship with someone bigger than yourself by taking the time to reconnect with what you find important about life and returning to the big questions of life.

Developing Compassion and Empathy

Empathy is the desire and inclination to truly appreciate another person's perspective and link it with your own. For instance, instead of treating an irritable co-worker as an annoyance, you can realize that they respond to occupational stress. Compassion is the discipline of responding with kindness to this understanding. You know that the co-worker is in a poor mood. You respond with extra compassion and listen sincerely as they vent, instead of snapping back. I am still working on this one.

Practise Forgiveness

It's not easy to let go of frustration, but the benefits of relinquishing bad emotions are abundant. Fred Luskin, the director of Stanford Forgiveness Project, advises having the best perspective to exercise forgiveness, examining whether your emotions originate from the reality of someone wronging you, or whether your frustration intensifies when you re-hash the case. See if you are influenced by certain impulses and let go of what is not beneficial. You don't have to re-establish touch with the one who has wronged you to apologize. Be gentle to yourself as well. I can honestly say that this isn't easy but it's worth it. I have personally been working through past pain, and it only affects me. We can't change the way or actions of another.

Practise Goodness With Yourself

Spirituality's nonphysical features can make it sound as if it is a distant activity, isolated from the rest of your life. But this is not true: spirituality is deeply affected by other variables in the lifestyle, much as the other facets of wellbeing.

One way to remind yourself that you truly care for this life and this body is to work out daily and consume a nutrient-rich diet of plenty of vegetables and fruits. It is very important to pay attention to what you eat. According to Jon Kabat Zinn, practising mindful eating "helps you to drop right into knowledge in ways that are uncomplicated, completely natural, and completely beyond words and thought." I also drink a lot of water as I know I often get dehydrated.

It is just as important to treat yourself with kindness as to treat others like that, says Kristin Neff. We change our bodies as well as our minds when we experience wet and tender emotions for ourselves. We feel relaxed, happy, trusting, and safe, instead of feeling worried and anxious. The expanding influence of these positive emotions will increase our sense of excitement, wonder, and awe, all feelings that lead to spirituality. I often say if you can't be kind to yourself, you really can't be kind to anyone else.

Start Practising Gratitude

We all have experienced those days, no matter how wonderful life is, when stuff just doesn't seem to be happening in the way we want it to, or when things come up that we need to focus on, and we're more vulnerable and just feel 'wrong.'

Your outlook starts to transform by ending the day with reflections of what you are thankful for, and you know that every day is genuinely amazing and full of blessings. All we have to do is take the time to enjoy them and free up space for so many more fantastic things to join our lives. This is a large part of working as a medium, as I have been blessed with so many things. The good has only come after the bad.

Start Taking Care of Your Body

Our bodies function in this life as a vessel of our mind and spirit. You must maintain your body working at optimum levels for your mind and spirit to function at maximum levels.

For multiple entities, this may mean various things. Don't give in or go gluten-free to the new food movement only because someone else is doing it. Learn how to listen to your own body. I was once asked whether I am vegan because I work with the spirit world. I had to remind them that spirit doesn't judge. The only person that can is me, after I have eaten things that don't work well with my diet. Chocolate and cheese are my own downfall, but the more I criticize and judge myself, the worse it becomes. If in doubt say Fuck it.

Your body knows best, and if you check in and listen, you'll discover a high-vibe lifestyle that's right for you, with a little experimenting.

Live the Life as You Breathe

Your breath is the centre of life for you. To be more mindful of your breath, make a promise. Intense moments, take care of how you breathe. Are your breaths rapid and shallow? Or are you taking absolute, deep breaths and allowing your whole body to flow with oxygen?

It is both healing and life-changing to practise taking absolute, deep breaths. It can be like trying to breathe all over again if you've spent most of your life as a shallow breather.

Learning to Breathe

The abdomen can stretch outward as you inhale, allowing your breath to spread fully across the bloodstream. It will make your blood more heavily oxygenated, which in turn will fuel your brain cells and muscles, allowing you to think more clearly. Your abdomen should contract inwards when you exhale.

Practise to Surrender Yourself

Pray, meditate, and surrender. This is the part in which you release the result's power and believe that life has your back and that it works for the best benefit.

Things always turn out a million times better than we could ever imagine when we genuinely abandon our attachment to the desired outcome.

You get to live in the flow when you submit to the larger life force within you. Put out the high vibes, do the job, and then believe that what comes to you is entirely, divinely fine.

Grounding

It's easy to get yourself wrapped up in all that's (or isn't) occurring around us as we go about our lives: our increasing to-do list, the what-ifs of the future, and wistful daydreams.

These fast-moving impulses drag us from the here and now, further and further forward. The act of linking yourself back to physical reality is called grounding. This teaches us to live in the current moment and be mindful of what is going on around us. When you feel disconnected from the "real world," grounding will help you change your attention and be aware of the here and now. I have shared earlier how I ground, but there are many ways to do this. Go with your heart.

Some people simply believe that you should go outdoors and walk barefoot, or lie on the grass to communicate with the earth and nature. While this is fantastic, and the experience will certainly benefit, it is not necessarily realistic or even feasible. For one thing, if it's the middle of winter, it's not the perfect time to walk outdoors barefoot!

Whether inside or outside, the steps can be done anywhere. Start by shutting your eyes and taking a few deep breaths. Keep your breathing very concentrated, and be mindful of both inhalation and exhalation.

When you feel ready, start visualizing that you have roots rising out of your body that bind you back to Earth. These roots grow stronger and deeper with each inhale, dragging you down into the earth. You can feel your body becoming heavy as these roots expand.

It might help to visualize your spirit (or soul, or whatever you want to refer to this concept!) being drawn back to your body if you feel yourself struggling. It was floating among the clouds before that, but it is drawn closer to your actual body with each breath. When you are relaxed and feeling like you are one with your spirit and physical body, it is time to move on to concentrate.

Centring

Each day, you go to work. You connect with clients all day long, trying your best to go above and beyond while serving them. When you connect with hundreds of individuals during your work day, you wear a winning grin and keep a great attitude. You have an angry client more than once, who is grumpy at you and just rude. You're emotionally and psychologically tired by the end of the day, and want nothing more than to sit in your pajamas with a movie in front of the TV.

This is why it's so important to centre!. I often add a fuck you in my head to these people, but you can be kinder.

Everything in the world is comprised of energy, including all of us. We give away fragments of our energy as we move through life and gather bits of others' energy. If we don't focus and concentrate on this energy transfer, we can find ourselves bearing the burden of others' dissatisfaction while losing substantial parts of our soul!

Centring is the process of adding back to your body the energy that you have given up, thus shedding from all else the energy you have accumulated. You restore harmony to the soul in doing so, and can pass through life more efficiently.

How To Centre

A vital aspect of centring is knowing where the energy source is. Take a few deep breaths with your eyes closed. You can feel, as you breathe in, all the energy you left behind in the environment rushing back to you. This energy will fill you up and return your soul to a state of fullness.

Envision that you are blowing away the extra rubble from everybody else on the exhale. All the harmful energy that has accrued is being neutralized and sent away within you, leaving you feeling free and light.

To help the process, you may want some sort of visualization. It is good to imagine that an empty cup or bucket, which can hold many litres, is your energy source. Your cup is slowly filled up with water (your energy) on each inhale, and the rubbish behind it (the energy of others) is being sent away.

Some other options may include:

- A rainbow puzzle of incomplete bits. Each inhales a piece to the puzzle, while pieces that do not match are sent away by the exhale.
- A book where positive claims are written on each inhale, while negative claims on the exhale are deleted.
- A greenhouse where each inhalation results in a blooming flower and certain weeds are removed with each exhalation.

Shielding

The process of defending yourself from energetic attacks or drainage is called shielding. Can you remember the job situation we pictured earlier? You would not have endured such a deep energy loss if you had adequately protected yourself before your change. You are essentially blocking all energy, that is not for the best or greatest benefit, from touching you by creating an energetic barrier around you. The negativity of others will not affect you as deeply. You're not going to feel that much of a burden from the chaotic energy of everyday life.

How to Shield Yourself

Begin by shutting your eyes and working up some energy for a moment. Focus on your energy core working, and sense the energy pulsating inside you. Take some deep breaths when you know you have drummed up enough power. When you breathe in, believe that you are packed with good energies from the breeze. Until you are full of good thoughts, you want to replicate this.

Next, you need this energy to concentrate. Try to take deep breaths, and picture the energy core opening up as you exhale. Visualize the momentum you've built up, spreading from it until you know it's available. This is the beneficial energy in the shield that will finally end up forming.

Take the time to understand the force the first few times you are shielded.

Identify as many features as you can:

- What colour are they?
- What's are they made of? Oh, light? Huh? Liquid? Anything entirely altogether?
- Are they hot or too cold?
- How are they getting around?

The better the visualization, the more efficient your shield will be.

Enable this energy to consume you completely. Imagine it creating a sphere of security around you. Reflect on the shield's purpose to allow only energies which are for your greatest and highest benefit. This can take a while, but it's worth it. The shield is, after all, just as powerful as you make it!. You can also continue trying new ways to shield yourself, or vary the amount of times that you do it in a day.

Spirituality And Sustainability

It is important to cut your energy centre when you're prepared. If you miss this, the energy that you don't want will be able to continue to pour freely from you.

You can picture the energy stirred up, breaking like a rubber band away from you, and then working on shutting your energy core until you can't see the energy streaming anymore. You'll be able to decide what fits best for you with some experience. Every day, you can use these three skills, and experience a tremendous change in your mental and moral wellbeing as a result.

At first, it might seem like a lot, but remember that practice makes it better! You'll continue to understand what works for you (and what doesn't) as you do these more often. These are also a perfect way to make the energy more familiar and help you learn to control it.

Mental Health And Emotional Problems

Depression is the most prominent mental health concern today, and has been the subject of much of the study that examines the connection between spirituality and mental health. There is information indicating a positive correlation, in parents, children, and young people, between church attendance and lower levels of depression. It also indicates that confidence in a transcendent being is related to decreased depressive symptoms. The connection between spirituality and anxiety or tension has been explored in related studies.

In various groups, quantitative evidence indicates decreased levels of fear, including later-life care patients, women with breast cancer, middle-aged adults with heart complications, and those healing from spinal surgery. Qualitative evidence further shows that changes in emotional wellbeing and anxiety decreases are also correlated with yoga and meditation. The connection between spirituality and post-traumatic stress disorder (PTSD) is explored in emerging literature.

Eleven studies that identified connections between faith, spirituality and mental health issues based on trauma were found in one review. I have told some people that I also have PTSD, and it's a daily practice of being the best I can at that moment but not giving myself a hard time when it's not a good day.

A report of these 11 studies achieves three key results. In the first place, the findings indicate that faith and spirituality are generally helpful to individuals coping with the effects of trauma, but not always. Second, they demonstrate that a deepening in faith or spirituality may arise from stressful experiences. Third, with increased post-traumatic healing, constructive religious coping, religious tolerance, ability to face existential problems, religious participation, and inherent religiousness are usually correlated. However, there is still relatively scant research discussing faith as it relates to schizophrenia.

One analysis of the literature suggested that "religion plays a central role in the reconstruction processes of a sense of self and recovery." Another found that religion can be a cohesive and supportive force for people who hold the same religious beliefs as their families.

I have mentioned many times that religion and spirituality can go hand in hand, as we believe in the afterlife, and that although we may use different wording there is a lot of similarity.

Not all studies investigating the correlation between moral or religious practice and anxiety reveals the former's positive effects on the latter. Rather, how spirituality is articulated seems to rely to some degree on it. Increased mental health conditions, for instance, are also seen in those with a strict religious education. Some also feel that their personal or moral values are not recognized or discussed within mental health facilities. For several, practitioners either completely disregard a person's inner life or treat their spiritual beliefs as nothing more than psychopathological manifestations.

The effects of spiritual practice for physical wellbeing have been recognized and recorded for over a century. Any form of spiritual practice at the most simple stage tends to help you live longer.

Practitioners view the relationship between spirituality and mental health as less specifically focused on the benefits. In a new study, 45% of mental health practitioners felt that religion could contribute to mental ill-health, and 39% believed religion could shield people from mental ill-health. This ambiguity is partly because the relationship between the two has not always been viewed as a good one. Freud referred to religion as "humanity's ultimate obsessional neurosis," and others claimed that the relationship between mental health, religion, and spirituality was "at best unpleasant and at worst non-existent."

One theologian believed that religion is the "last taboo" in spirituality, and many contend that this belief is supported in all medical textbooks and mental health programs by a lack of commitment to faith. This condition has begun to improve lately. In the last decade or so, theologians (usually focused on a Christian worldview) have begun to write at length about the relationship between mental health and faith, and practitioners in other fields, including psychology, neuroscience, nursing, and gerontology, are gradually debating the dissociation between the two.

In that case, survivors and professions lend their voices to the statement that mental health and faith are intrinsically connected, and that people should connect and benefit from each other in relation to both of these fields. For instance, the first national user-led study of its kind was undertaken by the Mental Health Foundation in 1997. It showed that over half of service users had some sort of spiritual conviction, and that these beliefs were meaningful and essential to them in terms of their mental health. Service users were then asked to explain their spiritual and moral interests.

In the discussions that resulted, religious values and practices included the meaning of guidance, a sense of purpose, comfort, grounding, enabling emotional suffering to be felt, and cultivating an inner love and sympathy towards others. Many of these are good for mental wellbeing. Generally, the emerging research reflects this change in viewpoint, and points to a protective or advantageous mental health influence of religion or spiritual practice.

Although this relationship shifts depending on how faith is represented or its components are evaluated, positive associations between faith/spirituality and general wellbeing, marital happiness, and general psychological functioning have been found. Similarly, some evidence suggests that some philosophical or religious experience can influence the mental health of those who suffer from depression, anxiety, post-traumatic stress, or schizophrenia, and we are now turning to that research.

Of course, it is very important to consider the shortcomings of clinical evaluation in terms of efficacy and comparability through various testing methodologies, experimental methods, etc., and relevance in terms of the real living environment of people while evaluating such research. Although understandably, experiments have been carried out regarding particular mental health conditions diagnosed, this naturally has some drawbacks in recognizing mental health and faith as a whole.

Depression And Spirituality

Depression is the mental health condition most often faced by people, and it presents itself in many forms and to varying degrees. It is characterized by one or more of a variety of symptoms, including feelings of sadness or suffering, unexplained exhaustion, and tiredness, the sensation that even the smallest tasks are almost impossible, lack of appetite for food or company, unnecessary worry, sensations like disappointment, unjustified feelings of shame, feelings of worthlessness or hopelessness, problems with sleep, and related ailments such as pain in back or cramps.

Depression affects 1 in 6 individuals at some stage in their life, and it is the subject of much of the study investigating the connection between faith and mental health. Nevertheless, it gives useful insight into the link between faith and other issues of mental health. John Swinton suggests that its very essence, frequently defined by feelings of hopelessness, loss of sense or intent in life, and poor self-esteem relates depression to what many people understand as faith. He outlines a small but in-depth observational study involving questioning six individuals who have had depression for at least two years.

The research aimed to create a rich explanation of their experiences, and discover the value of spirituality to those with depression. The importance of finding a sense of intent in life was one of the key concepts that resulted from the study. A temporary or stable disappearance of these elements of a person's life may be one of the distinguishing symptoms of depression.

For the participants in Swinton's research, this loss and its associated rediscovery were central aspects of both depression and spirituality. This represents what some in the literature have recorded, and what Philip Burnard has argued is the core principle in the meaning of spiritual treatment.

In questioning, uncertainty emerges about the matters that have previously given their importance and intent to a person. There are main aspects of life that, during depressive episodes, seem to vanish from view. Several religious and philosophical practices claim to give people significance and reason in the middle of an otherwise confounding or depressing life. Therefore, the capacity it provides to restore sense, direction, and hope to their lives may be one of the main contributions of spirituality in these individuals' lives.

In people with depression, one way in which significance can be restored from spirituality is through compassion and empathy. Understanding and empathy are the main vehicles by which depression can be alleviated for all the participants in Swinton's study and those in other user-led studies. While service users often say they feel confused by religious or mental health providers, they appear very strong when compassion and empathy are given.

Church participation is frequently (although not always) correlated with lower levels of depression for those who pursue value or reason in life through faith or spirituality, which is true for both parents, adolescents, and children. One way to explain this impact is to facilitate social participation (either unconsciously or actively) among some religious groups, which influences both depression and dealing with it.

Similarly, much of the evidence suggests that relative to those who join a church out of obligation or duty, individuals participating with religions that promote internalization of a series of beliefs are at significantly reduced risk of depression. One research showed a 70 percent rise in recovery from depressive symptoms after physical injury for every 10-point increase in the inherent religiosity of a person. Among those who believe in a transcendent being or greater authority and those who belong to a society of those who share their beliefs and give support, common results have been made.

Spiritual Growth And Development

The process of developing your inner self, your awareness, is spiritual development. It is a technique in which, through meditation, you awaken the spirit within and sense the energetic sensations within. Spiritual creation and progress allow you to feel better about yourself.

Our vision changes as we develop spiritually, and the way we see the planet around us often changes as well. A positive change in our lives brings about spiritual growth and development. In life, we not only become hopeful and happy but also become more stable and quiet. This progress encourages us to cope with the negativity surrounding us.

When we evolve spiritually, our outlook toward life in various ways often shifts for the better. Any of our concerns derive from our views of ourselves and the environment and our desires. You cannot be helped by philosophy and internal engineering to transform the universe, but it sure lets you change the way you view the world. One will know that this solves half of your life's problems. It has been said that a spiritual quest helps you see the world with a new pair of lenses!

Spiritual development and growth allow us to absorb humility. When we embark on a spiritual quest, the ego continues to melt away, jealously, selfishly. We become humble, generous, and nonviolent. If we have a modest outlook towards life, any event in our lives will teach us something. We will keep depression at bay while spiritually inclined, and spread the word of compassion and harmony around us. Our equations with people around us are shifting, we know. We respect partnerships, and a tendency to support others is also present.

Spirituality encourages us to create detachment, which contributes to inner peace. We learn to climb above disappointment and anger. Meditation, an aspect of spiritual development and growth, improves our physical wellbeing, enhances our focus, and sharpens our minds. A healthy lifestyle is driven by people who are religiously inclined. When we understand that this is connected to our spiritual development, a holistic approach to our lives and our overall emotional and physical being falls into play.

An increasing relation with God is often marked by spiritual growth, so prayers play an important role in spiritual growth and development. Chanting ancient scriptures also encourages us to find the harmony in our active, chaotic lives, which most of us lack. Keep reminding yourself that, even though you may not be religious, religion and spirituality can work side by side if you allow it.

Spiritual progress and growth allow us to gain a profound sense of who we really are, and how we can evolve internally. Our inner power and strength can increase exponentially.

Spirituality and inner harmony are a lifestyle. This encourages us to gain tremendous strength and bravery. It builds our stamina standards, and we can take full responsibility for our lives by living a life with no remorse, no shame, and/or no rage. To make people happier individuals, moral growth and advancement will benefit.

The Need For Personal Growth

We continue to discuss and argue how important personal development is for us. But do we know what personal development is? We still tend to equate monetary upscale as personal growth but believe that the personal word evolution includes far more than we might imagine, and certainly more than just an economic ladder increase.

Look at the world around you, and you'll see that we're all undeveloped people in person. Why am I saying that? You'll see crime, bigotry, sickness, and hate everywhere you look, and what does all this denote?

We should spare our own time to relax and reflect. We have to remind ourselves why this is going on. To change this negativity, what should we do? Might this be the reason why personal development is needed? Is it possible for us to do anything about it, then?

In our lives, we need personal development. The only one you can influence is yourself, and who knows, maybe the change can affect those around you. You cannot change other people; however hard you try, they will change only after being affected by you. You might be a little suspicious of this theory, but there is evidence. The confirmation is from a theoretical analysis known as The Law of Attraction and Quantum Mechanics. Thus, the Law of Attraction should address the question of why we need personal growth. The laws of quantum mechanics simply show that all objects are composed of material.

They are non-physical realities that in the physical world are not apparent yet. Since our thoughts and impulses are just energy, it suggests that whatever you concentrate your thoughts on creates your life. But as you dwell on thinking about the things you dread, the things you hate or don't like, you build and draw more bad things into your life. However, you draw a lot of it in excess as you spend your thoughts on the things you like or want. This is where professional improvement plays a role.

The energy pulls the same kind of energy as you think about positive things. You meet more people who are also optimistic and satisfied if the mind is focused on something positive and happy. The people who are miserable or unsuccessful around you will either step on or turn their feelings into more optimistic ones. This is precisely why we should have personal growth.

Developing Our Personality

Conflict is a situation when two or more persons have opposition, conflict, and/or antagonism. This may be considered as a lack of coordination, gaps in concepts, opinions, and feelings on certain topics, and/or inconsistencies. When conflicts emerge, people feel pressures, cold vibes, power struggles, wars, etc. Workplace disputes will hamper the success of the work and stun the organization's development in turn. Conflicts serve as obstacles to healthy organizational development. Still, though, no matter how much we try, we end up with contrasting feelings with team members. Therefore, conflict mediation is important so that it has a limited effect on our lives.

Unresolved disputes, especially at workplaces, can be risky. They can lead to unacceptable conduct, such as avoidance, teamwork failure, verbal attacks, and general frustration. In worse situations, some of the company's workers become so abusive that they finally have to leave their job and separate from the organization. It still shocks me when some people talk of their experience because I know the issue is actually themselves but they really can't see it, and they continue to blame others.

How do you handle disputes in a smart way? Communication is the best option. Openly share your views, feelings, and values, but do not ask everybody to agree with you. Be open to dialogue, conversation, and disagreements. You must note that this interaction is for the improvement of the mission or the work entrusted to you and your team members. Do not get intimate, therefore, and avoid hostility with the individual. Controlling your frustration is another point to consider. Use terms such as "I understand," "I agree with you slightly," "What you're doing is okay, but. .," and then bring the argument forward. This will change things and lead to a constructive dialogue that removes the space for disagreements.

Do not seek to settle disputes by non-personal means of communication such as emails or computer messages. This can escalate the situation. Listen to what the other person needs to say. You will add harmony and answers to the conflict if you listen and respond accordingly. For example, you have had a meeting over a new product launch with your team members and your manager, and you have said that winter is the best time to launch the product, but your colleagues do not think so. Allow them to talk, and ask them respectfully what the alternative solutions are. If you agree humbly with their points, embrace that. If you do not agree, outline and substantiate the reasons with examples. Ask any other staff members for input and let the head/boss know.

When handling disputes, containing your rage and resentment is the greatest difficulty. It's easier to be still occasionally and let the time slip by so that you can think more critically about things. Handling disputes does not mean being subordinate and listening to whatever people around you have to say, only to discourage conflicts. As you know by now, I am still working on how I deal with people who just don't get it and make excuses for their own decisions.

It is incredibly important to set forward your point and what you think. Good connectivity is indispensable. You can also try to keep your pride aside too. Hold no room for issues of the mindset of any kind. Be modest, wise, and a fantastic communicator and the rest is going to fall into place!. I know that this is easier said than done, but it truly can and does work.

Learn To Manage Stress

Many of us live a fast-paced and stressful life, coping with job pressure, home duties, and other obligations. At one time or another, we all cope with tension. This burden becomes part and parcel of our lives occasionally. It's incredibly necessary to handle tension, though. Stress has a lot of adverse impacts on the mind and body. People under stress often encounter headaches, anxiety, sadness, suicidal feelings, nausea, anger, resentment, etc.

Handling tension is also necessary in order to mitigate these issues. You may assume that there's nothing you can do about tension, but that's not exactly true. To keep stress under control, you need to work out daily. You need an improvement in your routine, and a sense of positivity has to be taught. You need to take responsibility for your opinions, emotions, and behaviour. This is a key point throughout my work with spirit as it is up to me. There have been many times I can't be bothered but if I don't do it, no one else will do it for me. It goes back to the ownership piece we talked about earlier.

Yoga, meditation, and breathing techniques are great ways of combating tension. The ultimate aim of stress control is to lead a happy life. In life, work is not everything. You need to take time for relaxation and recreational activity that will relax and soothe your mind. Some people use crystals, while others walk in nature. If you are unable to do either of these things, think about what else you can do. I remember being told in my childhood to count sheep in order to help me sleep. Strange I know, but it always helped me sleep.

Some individuals claim that by keeping a diary, you can manage tension. Any time you get stressed, write down what caused the stress. In this way, the objects and the entities that stress you can be identified. After a few days, you will know once you see this journal that some normal things stress you. Half of the work undertaken is to define these items.

Now, write down your reaction to the things that have stressed you out. You will understand that an alternative peaceful intervention will cause less tension. Write down that alternative action and what you should do if those situations happen again.

Smoking and drinking massive quantities of alcohol are some of the worst ways of dealing with tension. As an ex-smoker of 14 years, I recall how easy it was to just sit up and smoke when stressed, but I was lucky as I gave it up overnight when we adopted children. When you are depressed, stop eating or sleeping too long, as this will leave you limp. Stop several hours of pacing in front of the TV. Choose better ways to relieve the depression instead. First and foremost, to prevent undue tension, you need to coordinate and schedule your life.

For instance, plan your day in advance. Schedule meetings, be on time for them, get home from work on time, do not waste time gossiping, etc. To understand what is awaiting and how much can be done in a day, keep a to-do list with you. When planning this to-do list, be practical and set manageable expectations so there is no burden. Learn to say no. There is just so much you can do as a human being. Do not expect so much of yourself. Relax, rejuvenate and recharge yourself. The moment you start to see the patterns is when you should do something about it.

Combat Negative Thoughts

As human beings, we continuously face negative concepts such as rage, discomfort, tension, annoyance, anxiety, remorse, sorrow, grief, dissatisfaction, etc. Not only can negative emotions disrupt our emotional balance, but they can also affect our physical wellbeing. Depressive emotions are some of the hardest experiences we can encounter. It is not always easy to be optimistic.

Unpleasant thoughts can always sneak in and interrupt you. But here is where it works with the influence of constructive thought. Work to stop pessimistic feelings and cope with them instead of avoiding them. Face the uncertainty of things and do not fret in expectation.

We need to try to isolate and think like an observer from our negative feelings and emotions. Any of them can impact how we feel, as we have hundreds of thoughts every day. Fear of losing, fear of failing, fear of being alone, etc. are the main ones. Our subconscious pulls us into a whirlpool of destructive emotions, and we lose the harmony of life and our inner peace. We are being emotional and losing hold of our thoughts. Certain people continuously examine their emotions.

As this will still lead you to have negative feelings, you need to stop doing this. In your body, pessimistic thoughts will cause stress, and your subconscious will stop functioning. Bad ideas are often the product of worrying about what people say about you. People place pressure on themselves, not just because they have a sense of what others think of them, but because strive to become what they cannot. Not only does this contribute to negativity, but too much strain is generated! It is none of your business what people think of you. You must stay true to yourself.

Let the thoughts come as if you do not completely control them. Your ideas need to be compatible. When there's a bad scenario, let that be. Don't mull it over. Do not fight it or worry about it endlessly and get nervous. Know that certain aspects are beyond your grasp. Therefore, what you say in your head won't alter the situation. It would just hamper your mind without addressing the question. When any unpleasant thoughts come to your head, mentally brace yourself, become conscious of them, and most importantly, allow your mind, body, and spirit to become aware of them.

Bad thoughts are not something that can be deleted or erased by you. You need to learn to deal with them in such a manner that they do not in any way impact or harm you. Two main words are recognition and assimilation. And depressive feelings will show you too much, so the trick is to understand and acquire positive qualities from your negative thoughts. I think it's worth the reminder that most people have a touch of depression at some point in their life. It might have just been a day when they didn't get that job, or maybe a fall-out with a friend, or relationship issues. The most important thing to remember is that you are not alone, and that things will and can get better. It's the starting part you need.

Acknowledge The Power Of Positive Thinking

We all keep reading about the impact of positive thought, and how it will transform our lives, but it is often hard for us to maintain positivity and hope. Good thought should not be a compulsive habit but a way of life. Positive thought should not be viewed as a subject that needs to be taught. You ought to learn to be optimistic, of course, but it should not be viewed as a subject that you learn in school. Our mental health impacts our physical health, and constructive changes will also cause changes in our physical health! The strength of constructive thought is tremendous. It allows us to be stress-free, knowingly and unconsciously.

In changing our lives, constructive thought has a great deal of impact. So how can the productive transition in constructive thought be carried about? Positive thinking is the capacity to use our ideas in any situation, to visualize and expect the best possible consequence. As human beings, much of our problems derive from things we foresee, and the worst potential consequence is predicted more often than not. This is what has to be tweaked. For starters, if a student has worked hard for their exams and anticipates their outcomes, they would predict positive outcomes. Stop worrying about scores and grades.

A confident student will assume that they will get good grades because they have worked hard. Irritation and agitation may be generated by negativity, all of which are detrimental to the mind and body. Think optimistic, and life is going to be very lovely! Even the worst thing in life has a positive aspect.

For self-improvement and personality growth, the influence of constructive thought works well. Everybody needs to be connected to a good person around them. We have a good outlook, and we draw people around us. It strengthens our current state and contributes to a constructive life course. Strong behaviour allows us to imagine favourable environments.

We need to consider our talents, strong values, and constructive skills if we strive for self-improvement for our personal growth, and we need to be sure that we can fulfill our tasks and overcome what life gives us. To emerge as a stronger, positive individual, we must prioritize the positive character qualities we have and further strengthen them. Positive thoughts can help a great deal, even in a corporate set-up. People who hold leadership positions ought to be optimistic and spread confidence amongst the workers. When it comes to getting something done, constructive thought can be a great motivating force.

Here are some constructive improvements that you could adapt to understand the influence of positive thinking: Search for positive individuals to be aligned with it in any situation. Be a happier person at all times. When you wake up every day, you want to be cheerful and friendly. In life, be optimistic in your attitude. Disseminate pleasure. Never again let bad thoughts influence you. Think confidently, and there will be nice stuff going on. If you feel you're going to win, you will succeed because this is the strength of optimistic thought. I have said many times, if you are negative, negative things come. That's the law of attraction.

Find Happiness Within Yourself

Happiness is simply a state of mind in which you feel relaxed, satisfied, and peaceful. Much of us look outside of ourselves for happiness. We search for happiness in wealth, in people around us, in worldly things, but happiness is something inside us. Happiness achieved elsewhere is unstable.

Happiness in our personal lives is based on nothing other than the decisions we make. Above everything, we know that there is a greater self within us, which is above all else, as we look within and speak with our inner being. To be satisfied, this inner being does not need money or other things. In reality, the smallest things in our everyday lives will bring us happiness.

You can be really satisfied with a book, a smiling boy or girl, a few nice words, and other priceless items like these. Sadly, we are in a society that assigns a lot of value to worldly riches. However, this may make you prosperous, but it does not make you happy. Happiness resides inside us, and first, with our inner selves, we all have to be content. When we make a pact to be at peace with ourselves, our pleasure within will not be influenced by outside suffering.

Without a doubt, life is not a joyride, and it has its peaks and troughs. In our moments of sorrow and tough days, we all go through them. This is when inner harmony and joy allows us to deal with those tough times. No concerns can trouble us when we are satisfied from the inside. Nothing can worry us, and we are full of good energy that helps us cope with tough times. We always seek ultimate happiness as human beings, but desire is the root path of suffering. Happiness is a situation in which we have no need. Inside our mind and heart, it is a feeling that we are happy and we respect our precious lives in such a way that we do not want to spend time with unpleasant feelings such as rage, resentment, and sorrow.

Those who have achieved inner peace have claimed that they experience enormous quantities of good energy within themselves. They feel simple and light. Practising meditation is said to help you achieve inner peace. Do things from the inside that make you feel happy.

Generosity is one way to feel very fulfilled. You feel happy as you support the underprivileged and see the happiness on their faces. There is real pleasure here.

Your job should be compatible with your inner being to allow you to continually be in a state of happiness. You must truly know yourself and be mindful of your emotions, feelings, and actions. Find out what thoughts make you happy. Surround yourself with individuals that are content and promote positivity. Stop being in the company of actively cribbing persons who, in their approach, are pessimistic. Happiness lies internally, and to feel what it truly is to be satisfied, one must get in touch with it. No capital, no materialistic things, no worldly matters; the way joy is inside will bring happiness!

Inner Peace

Inner peace is a quiet, secure, calm, stress-free, and happy state, often referred to as peace of mind. It may not be easy to sustain inner peace in a hectic, fast-paced life, but we must all aim for a balanced state of being to promote inner peace. Not only does anxiety affect our physical life, but it leaves us emotionally ill. Mental relaxation, which can be accomplished by breathing exercises and meditation, can help you relax your mind and increase focus.

Seeking inner peace is often connected with spirituality, especially Buddhism and Hinduism. Both traditions lay a lot of value on mental stability and preserving inner harmony.

According to Buddhism, a relaxed person is closer to God than one who is emotionally depressed, angry, or annoyed. If you are used to an exhausting, and complicated lifestyle, you cannot reach a relaxed state of being in a few days. In your thinking and emotions, though, finding inner harmony is a matter of transition.

From the mind comes the preservation of peace within. You need to speak to your subconscious about the fact that it can't stress itself. Consider two words, 'inner harmony,' and take a deep breath any time you feel upset or annoyed. It'll make you feel lighter instantly.

Establish balance for whatever worries you. You may be annoyed, for instance, by the fact that your cleaner doesn't clean your house the way you like it. Speak to your cleaner, explain the cleaning part to him or her, and figure out the issue. However, inner happiness should not be disturbed by things like these and other bigger life issues. Many people continue to deal with problems that bring them distress and tension.

When you deal with your mind and heart to keep fears at bay and build peace inside, things get quite easy; most people find that things they are worried about are very trivial. Growing hyper, worried, and depressed was just their essence. They know that they are one step closer to finding inner harmony as soon as they decide to practise gradual changes in their lives. It is then that their thinking and behaviour change.

Change is constant, but it may not be so easy to change yourself and your habits. It should be a method that takes place step by step. Start waking up and doing yoga and breathing exercises early in the morning. Or, if you can't do that, spend a few minutes on yourself, reading a book and stepping outside. Try to stop running to get something. Be punctual and resist laziness. Allow enough time for leisurely pursuits and relaxation. It is really important to spend quality time with one another. Spend an hour a day by yourself where you are away from a cell phone, laptop, or networking system of any kind. Establish trust and persistence, which are all the mind's functions. Imagine a life of happiness and hold demands to a limit.

The Role of Emotions in our Lives

Emotions such as pleasure, loneliness, frustration, confidence, fear, remorse, embarrassment, guilt, joy, love, etc. are what we encounter within ourselves, based on our perceptions and the stimuli we derive from our environment and people around us.- Every person has a particular understanding of the case at hand, and every person experiences it differently. That is why it is felt that some people are more emotional than others.

For any definitive decision that we make as human beings, our thoughts are the main driving factor. Right from the moment we are born into this world, we experience feelings. When we grow up, we eventually begin to better understand the world around us and even develop a better sense of our feelings. Emotions are the main component of our existence, influencing our general being and actions. Whether it is anger, sorrow, pleasure, remorse, or something else, we are continually feeling various kinds of emotions. We do have to be responsible for those emotions, and what we can do about them.

It is very important to get a full grip of your emotions in order to lead a stable life. A significant part of understanding our addictions is the role of feelings in driving those actions. Addiction does not occur without feelings. Addiction does not occur without extreme desire.

We human beings live in a close-knit community in which our previous interactions influence our attitudes and acts. Any feelings of terror, rage, affection, and sorrow are so intense that they cause us to do things that we wouldn't even imagine doing otherwise. On the other hand, often people have a strong handle on their feelings These powerful and strong feelings are good, but letting them overwhelm us is evil. Our body secretes many hormones in conditions like this, which makes it impossible for our brain to make any decisions. Our judgments become skewed on those occasions, and we focus them on our previous experiences.

We get into despair as strong feelings surround us, so we become harmful, not just to ourselves but also to others. When we're mad, we don't know how our acts affect others, or damage our own bodies.

We have to exercise a certain influence on our feelings to get out of those circumstances. To face any emotional imbalance or disruption, we need to be solid. We need to consider emotions, and their role in our lives for this reason.

We ought to consider the degree to which we can take control of our feelings. Individuals who commit suicide have no power over their thoughts. They don't know that they're a prisoner of their thoughts. We need a solid enough brain and heart so that no feeling will take hold of us. This can be accomplished by cultivating interests, doing activities that satisfy us, instilling a feeling of hope and positivity around us, and practising meditation and breathing techniques.

The Different Stages of Human Learning

Human learning is an information development process. When we filter knowledge into our minds and understand it, our behaviour, talents, beliefs, and ethics are acquired. Human learning may occur as part of schooling, personal growth, or any other informal/formal training. When they play, explore, and communicate, children understand. The learning process, however, is a continual process. Via our experiences, we understand, unlearn and relearn. We need to learn to articulate thoughts, educate people, connect, develop, etc.

Four stages of learning are said to exist. Unconscious incompetence is a stage where something we don't know is not known to us. This means that, in this world, we are not yet conscious of such things. We have no understanding of the presence of intelligence of any kind. The person does not know how to do anything and does not accept this inherently.

Conscious incompetence is the second stage. This means we know what we're not comfortable with. Some phenomena exist and we are mindful of them, but we know consciously that we do not know anything about them. Although the person does not know how to do something, he or she is understood. At this point, the making of errors may be central to the learning process. For example, an entity knows he or she doesn't know how to drive.

Conscious competence is the third stage of learning. Here, people are mindful of the learning that has taken place. If we know, we know. The person understands or knows how something can be done. In this learning process, the implementation of the skill plays a key role. A lot of focus is required. Example: An individual knows that he or she can cook, and focuses on the process while they do that.

Unconscious competence is the fourth stage of the learning process. This means that what we know, we don't know. Even for a certain talent, we as humans have had so much experience that it almost becomes our second nature. And we will do this with the greatest ease. Consequently, when doing other things, the expertise may also be carried out—depending on who and where it was trained, other people could even be taught these skills.

Spirituality and being aware of your own self is also learning in itself, aside from the process and the phases of human learning. Human beings must learn to be respectful of their souls, and must acknowledge harmony within themselves. It is a method of lifelong learning. Meditation exercise allows you to act from your thoughts, feelings, and other inner qualities. Even Maslow's hierarchy of needs speaks of self-actualization, the last level of desire. Over everything, human learning has to do with adaptive behaviour. In time, to become our imagined perfect self, we need to understand, teach and relearn. For most humans, though, the realization of the inner self is the best learning.

Spirituality and Religion

There are substantial variations between the teachings of Christ and the practices of mainstream Christianity, between the teachings of Buddha and Buddhism, as practised today, and between Hinduism and what Krishna taught. Divisions between sects have evolved and have often led to persecution and even war. When you look at the darkest times in religious history, it is impossible to imagine that people would have strayed so far from the revered teachings of their great mentors.

The initial message was spiritual, but to differing extents, by mistranslation and misunderstanding, through the loss of spiritual meditation rituals, through the efforts of less developed people to hide spiritual ideas in dogma, and by religions developing into political entities, the spirit was distorted or destroyed.

There are mystic traditions within all the main faiths that contain many of the aspects of spirituality. Generally, however, they do not represent popular religion, and they have also been labeled as blasphemy in certain circumstances. Persecution has all too frequently rewarded the dissemination of those teachings.

Within our different faiths, we are left with a very ambiguous mix of theological reality and dogma. It is important to consider the actual distinctions between spirituality and religious dogma if we want to sift out the theological elements. These distinctions within modern religion have become distinctly distinct over time:

Spirituality is faith-based, which has a deity or eternal consciousness idea that is strongly evolved and logical. As in Judaism, Christianity, and Islam, theological dogma may be theistic or atheistic, such as certain forms of Buddhism, Shintoism, and even Communism.

Generally, dogmatic sects have either a poorly defined and irrational definition of heaven, or no concept of God at all.

Spirituality is non-dualistic, which usually implies that human life's purpose is to recognize that our social behaviour and God's eternal consciousness are the same, and to integrate our consciousness into infinite consciousness.

Many theistic sects are dualistic, promoting a fundamental distinction between God and the universe and the assumption that when one dies, human life aims to enter into a relationship with God and go to heaven.

By practising spiritual meditation or something similar, spirituality is realistic and can be learned and understood. The emphasis is inward, bringing the practitioner to a personal realization. On the other hand, religious denominations prioritize faith. While they prescribe various kinds of worship to individuals, much of the real practice is socially oriented, consisting of rites, celebrations, and ceremonies.

Spirituality is a preference of lifestyle, which is woven into every part of an individual's living. Generally, faith is a compartmentalized aspect of a human's life, practised mainly in temples and churches. And to the extent that it is true to its initial divine nature, religion can fulfill the proper function in freeing the faithful from ignorance and spiritual gloom.

People often ask me how much I meditate, and the answer is simple: not often enough. I don't personally feel that I need to meditate to connect to the spirit world as I know that they are always surrounding me. I find that meditation helps me when I am trying to clear my mind of daily chatter. I actually do it while driving with my eyes open. I concentrate on my breathing and ask spirit to remove thoughts that don't serve my highest good. Meditation can be so much fun, but remember, it you don't succeed the first time, try try again.

I have written and led several guided meditations, and have included one below. I have done both guided and music meditations, and I have found that simpler is better. Meditation can be a lot of fun, but please remember the word fun.

It is best to read the following meditation several times and then record it. Please remember you can re-record it any time and change the prompts within.

To start please all take a drink of water, close your eyes and take a deep breath, release, take another and release and take one further breath and let go of your cares and worries.

Let's all visualize our umbilical cords growing from our bodies and connecting as one.

Continue to breathe like this, slowly and deeply, as you become more and more relaxed.

Visualize yourself walking on a path, made of sand, feel your feet sink into its golden warmth. Wiggle your toes and savour the sensation.

The path is long and winding. It is lined with tall undulating conifers, reaching towards the golden sunlight. Breathe in the rich green smell of the needles.

Look at the flowers, nodding in the midday breeze; the sunflowers bobbing in the breath of the wind.

Savour the rich butter yellow of the wondrous petals. Let your heart lift in the wonder of Mother Nature.

As you continue to walk along this path, it changes from sand to soft green grass. Feel your feet connect with each blade.

You hear the birds singing and calling to each other, messages of love and hope; the cardinals and yellow finches seemingly dancing against the blue bowl of the sky; the vivid colours of the bright reds and yellow merging like a daytime comet streaking across the sky.

You continue to follow this path, savouring the sweet soft grass beneath your feet. You feel the wind brush against your cheeks, and Mother Earth's warm embrace surrounding you like a cocoon.

You reach a meadow, filled with wildflowers, wild poppies and daisies as far as the eye can see.

The buzzing of crickets fills the air, and the soft buzz of a bee, drinking the sweet nectar of the open buds.

You find a small soft clearing, where you sit down and connect with Mother Earth. You place the palms of your hands face down and feel your fingers entwine with each blade of grass. Feel the warmth of the soil beneath you and the rays of the sun kissing your cheeks.

As you sit here, in this calm and peaceful place, your worries and cares drift away on the waves of the soft breeze.

A rabbit comes to you, and sits down next to you. You admire the fragile beauty. Its long, limber limbs, the frantic beating of its heart.

In a heartbeat it vanishes into the tall grass.

In the distance you see a figure approaching. As this figure gets closer, your eyes meet and a feeling of familiarity falls across your thoughts.

They sit next to you and you realize it's someone from your long distant past that has walked with you, laughed with you, cried with you and guided you. This is your spirit guide.

As you sit and enjoy the natural splendour of your surroundings, you ask their name, and your heart whispers across your thoughts.

You look at each other and smile, savouring this connection. Your lips move, but nothing comes out. Instead the conversation seems to be from within, where words are felt rather than heard.

Your wonderful wise guide gives you a gift. This gift is very special. You open it and give thanks. This gift is something that you will always remember.

It's time for your guide to leave, as they have other journeys that they need to take. As they get up and leave, their wise words stay with you.

It's time for you to leave this special place, remembering what you have been given. You stand up, the sunlight crowning your head. You begin your journey back along the path, through the meadow filled with wonderful sights and smells, the feeling of the soft fingers of grass caressing the soles of your feet, the energy running like a current pulsing to the very heart of you.

You continue to walk along the path and you come back to the golden sands. You have a sense of peace and calm, and also the gift from your guide.

When you are ready to leave this peaceful place, slowly begin to reawaken your body.

As you reawaken, keep with you the feeling of calm, peace, and relaxation.

Wiggle your fingers and toes to wake up your muscles.

When you are ready, open your eyes and return to your centre and awareness, feeling alert and refreshed.

Visualize roots coming from your feet to connect you back to Mother Earth.

Face Challenges

We all face difficult and tough times. Yet what makes our lives is how we face and cope with those challenges. Life throws several challenges at us as we grow up. As a student, every exam is a challenge. It is a challenge to develop a future and excel in life. Learning from mistakes is a challenge. Managing personal tragedy is a challenge. It is also a challenge to sustain a job and family. Therefore, we need to keep a good outlook and a never-say-die mentality as the secret to meeting all these diverse obstacles of life. Mentally, our emotions, values, and thoughts have a profound influence on our attitudes and behaviour. We feel happiness and wellbeing whenever we are optimistic.

Poor feelings drag us down, tending to make us feel depressed and sad. One of the most frequent questions people ask as they are going through stressful times is "Why me?" The answer to this question is that you are not the only one who is facing tough times.

Everyone has a share of concerns of their own. Some may have financial concerns, others may have difficulties relating to employment, and others may have some personal issues. All of us face obstacles of varying kinds. Some explain it, while others don't. However, what is crucial is to cultivate the right mindset to meet these challenges.

Developing a positive mind and retaining the emotional quotient (EQ) allows us to meet obstacles of every sort. There is no denying that some of the tough challenges we are living through are difficult to come to grips with. Individuals afflicted with cancer and attending rehabilitation must go through such tough periods. We want the help of friends and family members at times like this, who give us the confidence to face those tough times.

It is said that in recognizing the greater sense of life and meeting difficulties, both faith and meditation help a lot. We are supported by deep breathing, meditation, and workouts to alleviate our tension and become mentally and physically strong. Self-healing is important. Via constructive thoughts and peace of mind, this happens.

Getting our support structure in place is another means of meeting challenges. Establish good relationships. Friends will help you solve your issues, and it makes life easier to have their love. Members of your family will also offer support and inspiration to face a challenge of some sort. Gain not only through your encounters but also through insights with others. The challenges we encounter in life make us better, and help us learn about concerns so that we do not have to experience them again. Know that the only way to deal with a challenge is to overcome it, and learn from it.

Finally, predict the unpredictable from life, and you will learn that you are powerful enough to conquer any obstacle. Build the never-say-die spirit, and you will see that even with challenging times and daunting struggles, life is beautiful.

Keep Yourself Motivated

We lead really busy lives, and it's a challenge to keep enough excitement for the smaller things in life. The push is a relentless one, and is attacked by pessimistic feelings and fear about the future nearly every moment. Facing uncertainty and sadness isn't rare. Yet, the capacity to keep pushing on is all that keeps us alive.

To remain inspired, we have to consider our feelings, and the bond they share with our emotions. Understanding how to nurture motivating emotions, neutralize destructive ones and rely on the job at hand is of the utmost importance. It is important to dream of the future, but the present is of no less importance.

Sometimes, for reasons such as lack of self-confidence, lack of strong vision, and lack of proper guidance, we lose inspiration. When put together, all three items become fatal to our inspiration quotient. We have to keep track of all three factors to resolve the disabilities they cause, in order to empower ourselves.

You can inspire yourself by increasing your trust in yourself. Forget about your previous mistakes, terrible breaks, and your mind's dominating personal shortcomings. Never be jealous of your rivals, but strive to become the best version and live your best life instead. You should still stop finding reasons why you are unable to perform. Gratitude can still be the priority. Set aside time to reflect on something good in your life. Give your talents, previous contributions, and current rewards a proper mental list. Often, we take our successes for granted and reflect on our shortcomings, but it's important to make room for life's positivity instead. This unintentionally rejuvenates our confidence and motivates us so that we can expand on our existing performance.

Motivate yourself by giving guidance to your emotional thoughts. If you don't give them a sense of purpose, your plans and tactics are of no value. Identify the operations which lead to success.

Do all of this, and you will inspire yourself to wonder and marvel at yourself. I have written many affirmation statements to remind myself that I am loved, I am supported and I am not alone.

Chapter 6

Psychic Development: The Easy Way or Hard Way Depending on What You Do

We are all born with psychic skills. Some of us are intuitive and can rely upon our talent at will, and some do not understand anything about our psychic ability. Most people are somewhere in the middle. They have intuitive impulses or signals that come and go but have minimal or no effect over them. The argument is, deep inside, we all have psychic gifts, whether or not we notice them or know how to use them.

It's important to keep your psychic links open no matter where you place yourself: self-natural, weekend warrior, or novice. As with everything else, you can get rusty if you do not practise, and you do not trust.

Have a Practice Instrument

Tarot cards, runes, stones, pendulums, divining rods, and so on are psychic instruments or divination tools with which you can try to connect to the energy of the spirit world. With a series of directions, most will come. Regularly, start training with your equipment. Experiment with various instruments. Try a couple of assorted tarot decks or runes, etc. Initially, you might want to borrow a deck or a pendulum so you can check them out first, but in my experience many people buy their own in a short time.

I don't see it as bad to practise with other people's tools, but get permission and make sure that they are cleansed. You're going to discover that those are simpler for you to deal with. Everywhere you go, take your chosen items with you. You never know when you'll get the chance to train. Place them at night on your bedside table to communicate with them as deeply as you can.

Learn To Predict

Try predicting events every day, such as who's going to try to meet you that day. What bills or cheques are going to land in the mailbox? Try to show the details in the mail carrier's pocket. What colour is the envelope? Try first to listen to who it is and what they want any time you get a phone call, text, or email. Check the precision, then.

Try to anticipate your favourite sporting event's results. Visualize the rivals and try to appeal to their resources. Which athlete or which team feels better? Start "finding people" by dreaming about someone who you know well, and trying to find their focus. Are they on the job? In your grocery store? In the home? Ask them later where they were when you were "looking" for them. To gain faith in your talents, these basic practice exercises will give you the immediate guidance you need.

Practise On Family, Friends, and Colleagues

Find any open-minded people with whom to work. No matter how foolish they can sound, tell them the first thoughts that come into your mind. In cultivating your instincts, trust is one of the first and most relevant ingredients. Try working with new people until you feel relaxed working with anyone you meet. This is good practice because any pre-conceived notions you have about the photos, texts, or thoughts you get are not from the individual. (Instead of walking up to total strangers in the driveway, you might want to practise on people who are friends of someone you already know!) I used to say that I wouldn't walk up to people and start talking spirit but the word that soon changed . Oh well.

I have done it so many times I can't count anymore. All have received the messages given except one lady. I was at a mediumship event and I was sitting in front of a lady whose spirit kept on telling me that the mother was there, and that she had died of cancer, as well as some other information. I turned around and asked if I could share something with her, and she said that she was there only to receive a message from the person that was on the stage. She said she didn't understand the information as her mother had died of cancer. I looked up to the ceiling and said. I can't fix stupid. The lady never did get her message that day.

Keep A Journal

And if you think it's ridiculous and don't know what writing one means, write down your thoughts and feelings and emotions that enter your mind when you are with people. Make a point of pointing to your prose. Look through the entries later on, to see if anything makes sense that previously did not make sense.

The most crucial part to remember about psychic growth is that you know how to do it now! You are just waking the psychic force inside you that has been lying dormant. And even if you are unsure how to view them, the pictures, emotions, and messages you receive are right for you. The teachings within this book will help you learn more about your psychic style and how to interact with the energies that flow through you. Journaling can be fun. I personally don't see it as a requirement to write endless amounts; it could be just bullet points or statements.

Grounding and Preparing Yourself

Therapists, intuitive, and psychics all work with power and need to understand how to "ground" themselves. Meaning being bound to the ground or anchored, the word is loosely used. You feel relaxed, safe, solid, and concentrated while you are grounded. You need to remember that you can feel dizzy and out of contact with reality when interacting with energy. It is also important to learn how to ground yourself to "come back to earth" when you are done.

Before you start doing psychic practice, you must clear yourself so that you are comfortable and in charge, and you need to know how to restore your sense of personal equilibrium afterward. Learning how to ground yourself is like knowing the way home before you start on a long trip. It's a way to turn off the psychic switch and let the psychic world go, so that you can go about your everyday life without getting disturbed and disconnected from the overwhelming energy that you often experience when reading.

Since you can get overwhelmed, forgetful, and out of touch, being ungrounded can have detrimental consequences on your everyday life. So be careful and spend some time learning about this subject, please!

Your body and energy system automatically cleans out and opens up while you are calm and at peace. You can obtain psychic knowledge while the energy stream is uncluttered. The more space that you make within yourself, the more learning and growth you can do. It's all about the learning.

Growing Your Energic Roots

If you want to perform the exercise on your own, perform the Grounding Meditation recording:

1. With your hands on your legs, sit or stand calmly.
2. Take a few long, steady breaths.
3. Imagine that you have roots rising from the soles of your feet into your thighs, down into the soil, anchoring you.
4. Continue to concentrate on digging into the soil with your roots until you are cool and relaxed.

Wearing Or Carrying Grounding Stones

It will help you to ground yourself with hematite, carnelian, jasper, tourmaline, tiger's eye, smoky quartz, or other black or reddish stones. Wear a grounding stone or hold it in your bag or a pendant or other piece of jewelry. Clean the stone and concentrate on its solidity. I used to carry more crystals than I do now, but I think this has to do with the people I was around. I still have a lot of crystals at my home.

Set Your Intention

Before and after an attempt at psychic activity, it is necessary to create a purpose or say a safety prayer. It is, therefore, important for the process to strive for results.

Tools that help centre your strength and open you up are the habits or routines you create. You must trust strongly in yourself and your success. Set the readings for an optimistic purpose. This means that, during the process, only positive energies pass through you. A simple prayer or an affirmation you believe deeply will be adequate.

Use it before you start, or make your own if you have a favourite prayer of protection.

Smudging

Before you begin working, another way to manage a room and set up a positive work environment is to smudge the room. Smudging is a process that can be traced back to ancient times and is now used as a means of clearing energy by many aboriginal cultures and energy healers. In their services, many churches use incense as well. Shops like my own sell smudging products that can be bought, or you can make your own. It is possible to use any plant or herb that can be dried and burned to produce smoke, but historically, common plants and herbs are sage, sweetgrass, and cedar.

People sometimes dry and use sage from a garden, but it doesn't smell as good as any of the smears that have been professionally prepared.

They can be put loosely in a bowl or shell and set alight if you are using loose leaf herbs. Then blow the fire out softly because the herbs are still burning. If a smudge stick or braided sweetgrass is used, ignite one end and blow the flame out so that it can burn.

Using a feather or your hands, move the smoke over yourself until the smudge is smoky. Brush the smoke in the front and back of your head and neck. As you move the smoke, say a prayer or statement such as, " I ask any negative energy of spirit that doesn't serve my highest good to please leave and fill this room with love and light." I also repeat this many times as I am walking around the home or building. I am smudging. Go on wafting the smoke all over yourself. You will get the whole home finished. Pay careful attention to the corners, windows, and doors.

It is your strength and purpose that makes this happen, remember. Smudging has a strength that is known, and it is something that has been used for centuries by ghosts and forces around you. It contributes to your strength and your capacity to effectively use it.

Remember to be grateful for the safety that you get. Having simple intentions is analogous to the discipline of vigorous grooming. You can end up accumulating energies that are unhelpful, deceptive, and unsafe for you and others you are trying to help if you fail to set a good goal, or to clear your room. Bad energy appears to be accumulating in the corners like dust bunnies!

Remember when smudging, as I will repeat within this book, it's about intention whether you use sage, incense, or singing bowls. I have found when young people learn how to cleanse their own space early, it allows them to control their own environment.

Your Psychic Style

When working on your psychic ability, the next thing you need to be mindful of is that each individual has their specific way of obtaining knowledge. This is referred to by some sources as your psychic form or your intuitive style. When you start to gather information, you will obtain it in a way that makes sense to you as a person.

For example, some persons are visual learners, some are vocal, and some are hands-on, interactive learners. If you like to read and look at pictures or graphs, you will be more likely to obtain visual knowledge. You're more of an auditory learner if you like listening to presentations or verbal orders.

You are more of a physical learner if you feel the urge to explore and tamper with things. People who obtain dreams are clairvoyant of the intuitive realm. Clairaudients are people who receive messages, and something called psychometry is used by those who are tactile.

Clairvoyants, with their eyes either open or closed, may receive visions. When they are reading, they may want to have something to look at. Typically they prefer tarot cards or runes in the cards, for the symbols and the gestures on the faces. Clairaudients are listening to calls. They may be audible signals received with the ear, or they may sound like a little voice inside, but they may somehow know it as their inner voice.

By holding a person's hand or one of their items, psychometry includes getting details. Psychic types are classified into four major types: emotional, physical, psychological, and spiritual.

The Self

The self, simply put, is in its entirety the human psyche; it is the container that holds all of the parts and roles of the mind.

The unconscious aspect of the human mind is dynamic and has various levels, Jung claimed. He thought that each human had a special personal unconsciousness that included personal memories and feelings repressed, overlooked, or ignored. Jung referred to "feeling-toned complexes" that occur within each individual's unconscious, which are the emotions and impressions that you have about the important individuals and events in your life.

At first, all of this may seem a little overwhelming, but it is intended to make you aware that there is more than one way to be psychic. You will have more strategies that you can use, and more ways to boost your odds of success, as you encourage yourself to open up to the various ways you can use your instincts.

As a psychic being, you can still think you are a bit of a mixed bag. You can encounter a mixture of various stimuli. What often happens at first is that you get little flashes of knowledge, like pieces of a puzzle.

If you're lucky, you'll get enough pieces to make a picture. Do not stress about the fact that it takes a lot of practice to do this part. You can start to pretty quickly pick up on items, but it might take months or even years for you to understand how to correctly analyze the details. Starting this path with a strong determination and the aim of achieving is quite important. This we will all do. At your speed and in your own time, you will continue.

You may see fuzziness or light around a human, for instance, or you may feel that you see flashes of light or colour when you shut your eyes. Around the same time, anywhere in your hands or the back of your neck, you might get an itch.

This could all refer to pressure or pain somewhere in your body, and you could even have an emotional response. All in all, it means something. The crucial thing is to understand how to contact your psyche and body so that the wisdom that comes in can be picked up. The challenge after that is to figure it all out. It is also a challenge not to take it on yourself, within your own body.

Keep it easy in the beginning. You will have to keep reminding yourself of this point. Wanting to know all the answers is a normal human reaction. Now we want clarification. We want a step-by-step handbook and, yes, a signed promise!

Yet you've got to have patience. You may want to deal with people who are open to you, asking questions about them and sharing information until you feel comfortable with sharing information with strangers. To help you learn how to be a success, you need input. You will begin to link the feelings that you feel to what the Spirit person is telling you.

For you, those dreams or thoughts will begin to make sense. You can have a vision of an individual in a lab coat; for example, it reminds us that the entity is in a field where people wear lab coats. You will know they're in the area of medicine. This is a sign that I see when I want to talk about someone who is a doctor, nurse or PSW, or involved in medicine in any way. The key thing is that your system of clues and tips that make sense to you will be established.

Getting Started

Now for the interesting stuff, and it may be fun for you, truly! It should be entertaining and thrilling to grow your instincts. Initially, aim to keep things light and work on fewer and less meaningful tasks. As the first test of your psychic ability, you do not want to take on a missing person's condition, so try to select simple tasks such as those mentioned in the introduction section. Remember the worst that can happen when you are just practising... the words fuck it.

I was working with someone who was just starting out and they thought the best thing that they could do was work with missing people. I tried to explain that they needed to start at the beginning, but they had to learn their own lessons. They found that the emotions that go with spirit started to overwhelm them, and they ended up taking a step back. They found their own journey, and now they are in such a different place. It was about trust, and protecting themselves.

Spirit also has a habit of calling people out on their own gifts, and reminding people of what is possible. I have had the pleasure of working with many mentoring students who are doing their thing; some just use it to work alongside their own business, others just for themselves, and others are working as full-time mediums.

Hopefully, you will have a peaceful room, free of clutter and disturbances, to work in. It should be comfortable and warm, but it should not be so cozy that you fall asleep! This does happen more than you think. There are so many ways in which to practise with spirit, and it will be trial and error, but please ground and protect yourself before starting, Some people that I have met in my journey prefer to work with spirit at night, others in the morning. It's about finding your own jive.

Psychometry

Two terms are derived from psychometry: psyche, indicating "the soul," and metron, which means "to measure." Psychometry is the capacity to measure the soul. There are many types of psychometry. The most widely used methods include holding a person's hand or one of their items to calculate their energy and gather knowledge.

Regularly, we use psychometry without ever understanding it. We often calculate and gain knowledge about our surroundings, and the people or objects around us, through our personal energy fields and intuitive senses.

Have you ever had a particular feeling but were unable to articulate why you felt it? Emotions from other entities, or from items that others have handled, may be picked up. If you start having feelings of no known reason or cause, it may be the emotional vibrations left by others in the area.

Depending on our environment, we sometimes experience varying stimuli inside our bodies. We have one series of stimuli while we are in a position we interpret as stable or relaxed. We have a very different response when we are anywhere that we consider risky. It is important to pay attention to any hints and emotions you become conscious of while studying psychometry, particularly when you cannot quickly understand things.

Psychometry Exercise

Have anyone send you an item about which you know nothing? Real materials, such as metals, stones, paper, timber, etc., are typically simpler to deal with. There may also be a photograph included. Do not even look at it. Keep shutting your eyes. You may want them to give you something which is not theirs. You will have no preconceived notions about the object if you have no idea who the owner is, and the information you collect will be entirely different.

Ground and Clear. Take a few long, steady breaths and remind yourself that this can be done! Open up to believe.

Maintain yourself by holding the object.

Without looking at it, take care of the physical features you sense, such as scale, form, texture, weight, etc.

Observe whatever emotions you have. Pay attention to all the senses, visual, sensory, and physical. Look at the object when you are ready. If it is a person's image, look at their face. Keeping the item up to your third eye can be helpful. Document all thoughts, dreams, and texts. Some people feel that their relationship is disrupted by stopping to write stuff down, so you might want to make an audio recording. Experiment to discover what suits you best.

Attempt to dig at the object's past. Try to think about where it comes from, how old it is, and how many owners it may have had. Document your emotions and ideas. (Hint: Most users find that they can gaze at the past when they turn their eyes or head to the left, and they can peek into the future when they move their eyes or head to the right. You can do it either with your eyes open or closed.)

Try to assess the object's present need. Who is the new proprietor? Are they male or female? Try to figure out what the person looks like. How old do you think they are? How are they using the object? Who's been offering it to them? Have they bought it themselves? What kind of feelings have they had lately? For them, is this object meaningful?

If there are any signals to relay, ask the entity or any beings that accompany it. Take time to see what's coming up.

Try to see into the future that surrounds this piece. Make sure to note any emotions, feelings, dreams, or sounds that might occur. They always make sense or may become clearer to the owner later on.

Get feedback! Find out how you've done. Note that everybody gets details differently, and you can misunderstand the message if anything is incorrect. You may be receiving details that the owner knew about a former owner or others. Regularly repeating this practice will allow you to remember your strengths and improve your accuracy.

Remember to practise, practise, practise.

Some Variations

Check out a picture of somebody you know but haven't talked to lately. Keep it and log everything that you're feeling. Try to imagine what they are doing and what they have been up to. Then call them to find out how they've been doing recently.

Keep a letter, card, or postcard that another has written. As described above, do psychometry and then contact them. You can print an email, but it is easier to get one that has reached the user. Get together with friends and make everyone write the same sentence on a sheet of paper. As compared to "I hate cloudy days" or "I love the sunshine," be sure to make it an emotionally balanced expression such as "I saw a cloud" or "It is sunny outside." Gather the papers and then hand them out randomly. Get psychometry done by all and write down their experiences. Get each person, then attempt to decide who wrote on their piece of paper. Compare to see how everyone is going.

Collect three stones or crystals that are identical in size and form. Do one of them for psychometrics. Get your experiences registered. Interacting with crystals can be an enjoyable practice since they can deliver insightful healing messages. Then, drop the stone or crystal with the other ones in a bag or under a cloth and be careful to shuffle. Ask it to tell you which one it is and see if, without looking, you can pick it from the party. Trust your own feelings and thoughts.

Treat your plants with psychometry. If they need more water, less water, more sunlight, more fertilizer, etc., they will tell you. You will get around science by purchasing and planting two plants of the same size and type in the same location. Then, by catering to its desires as it talks to you, perform psychometry on one plant for a few months. Meanwhile, in your regular procedure, care for the other herb. See which plant grows larger. Just a fun way to use energy and see how it can work.

Do animal psychometry. Write down any contact you perceive. It's a bit difficult to get feedback, but you can track improvements in behaviour. Usually, animals respond by being relaxed, safer, and more affectionate if they are "listened to."

Intuitive Tools

For decades, intuitive instruments have been used to assist psychic and perceptive talents. To help them determine when to plant and when to reap their crops, ancient tribes depended upon them. Every person is different and what world for one person will not work for another.

On the Egyptian pyramids, there are pictures showing dowsing. Scrying tools, runes, and ways of dowsing have been used for thousands of years. As far back as the 12th century, tarot decks have been dated. As a short introduction, we are going to split these instruments into four categories.

Tarot Decks

Tarot decks are common to most people. Hundreds of different decks with different themes have been made. The majority of them contain 22 arcana major cards and 56 arcana minor or numbered cards (just like typical playing cards).

Rune Casting

Runes are common stones, bones, shells, or sticks bearing pictures from ancient alphabets that have been carved or drawn. Rune casting requires posing a question and casting them from a bag or under a fabric on a surface, or picking them. There are common meanings of each of the runes. Runes can be more difficult for people to start with but you could also create your own.

Scrying

Scrying refers to any procedure that includes concentrating or looking at a tool to receive pictures or messages. The idea is that it is always sufficient to channel knowledge while the mind is keenly concentrated on one task. Nostradamus was a prominent scribe who, in the 16th century, wrote many predictions. Examples of scrying involve gazing at a single stone, looking at a crystal ball, looking at fire or candle flames, looking at smoke or mist images, and peering into a water mirror or bowl.

Divining

Dowsing or divining of any object that may point or drag is performed. The instruments most widely used are dowsing hooks, sticks, or pendulums. Dowsing rods and pendulums are constructed from various materials, but it is typically simpler for the natural ones to transfer electricity. Throughout the globe, many dowsing communities meet, learn, and work together.

Choosing Your Tools

You can make a pendulum yourself out of a necklace or crystal but sometimes people like to purchase their first. Remind yourself what feels good and which is the best one to use, and remember to cleanse it.

When purchasing a new one, hold it in your hand. Look carefully at the object and take note of how it looks when you are keeping it. Are there any tingles or feelings you get? To figure out if the tool has any details for you, you might want to do some quick psychometry.

If it's a tarot deck, ask if you should look at the pictures by moving through the cards. Most come with a journal. Peek into the journal to see how the writing style appeals to you. Try the inner wisdom to trust and choose by intuition. Leave and return another day if you are not confident. Next time you look, you can find a great fit. There isn't any hurry.

Caring For Your Tools

Crystals favour open areas where they can consume sunshine and moonlight, so if you find that, once it has been used, you want to hold a crystal in a special location, go with the intuition and check it out.

Try to periodically pull the crystal out if you have not seen it for a long time. With non-use, and from a lack of new, open air for long periods, crystals become rusty.

Crystals, pendulums, and dowsing rods of metal should be washed from time to time with water and placed on a window sill under moonlight or sunlight to charge. Some crystals, such as selenite or desert rose, can't be washed. Some crystals are more brittle than others and may tend to break down over time.

Tarot cards should be shuffled to spread the energies before each reading. If you want to be associated with your tools, take them with you wherever you go. It is commonly advised that you cover them with a natural fabric or bag for tarot cards, runes and mirrors so that they do not suck up the ambient energy. I have wrapped my cards in old fabric napkins.

Some people tend not to let someone else, even for reading, touch their instruments. You might notice that you don't mind letting people touch your instruments and tools, but you will want to try to feel the entity in advance. You should clean your tools. A neurological link to the tools exists. You will find that you continue to open up to obtain knowledge as soon as you go through the ritual of treating them. At home, my family has over ten different decks. Some don't "speak" to me anymore and others, I just use for me. I use one deck most often, which I love, and I have just created a new one.

Must Do's Before an Exercise (Ouija, Tarot, etc.)

Remember to do the grounding and clearing exercises as preparation before you start. Make sure that you develop a strong mental goal to strive for the greatest good. In reading, you want to draw only positive energy.

It is smart to write your goals down, and have a pen and paper or tape recorder ready to document what pops up if you have any concerns that you wish to answer. It is very normal to miss a reading experience within a few minutes of completion.

Keep in communication with the people you are dealing with if you can, and encourage them to give you input later. There is nothing more confidence-boosting than finding out that something has come to fruition that you saw in a reading.

When you stop, give thanks for all the knowledge you have received, and release all the power. Ground yourself again.

Tarot Card Exercise

Do not try at first to recall the meanings of the cards or their suits. Reading tarot is an in-depth process that requires much research. This exercise aims to help you determine if you want to deal with tarot cards before investing in a package. Borrow a deck to work on, if possible, to figure out if you want to spend cash on your own deck. Tarot decks can be very costly. A perfect way to do this activity is to get together a group of friends and invite them to take one or two decks with them. You can try multiple decks that way and even work with several different entities to test your ability.

You may want to think about the essence of tarot cards before you get through the exercise. Cards are a wonderful way to help you make associations, but try not to take the cards' meanings more seriously than your own experiences of them. You're improving your skills at this stage, not memorizing a lot of definitions.

There are certain tarot cards with unsettling photos and sinister-sounding titles. Any deck has a death card, and typically a portrayal of the devil and some other bad looking characters. If you draw these cards, don't fret. Tarot cards are symbolic and typically are not literal images of things to come.

Death, for instance, is an ending that does not mean life's death. The death of a circumstance, a business, a work, or an unfortunate conflict is also symbolized. Death is always followed by regeneration and constructive development. The demon signifies temptations and difficulties. Everyone has problems in life, and reading can also make people more conscious of future pitfalls, and ways to escape them. A reading will also help a participant understand a difficult situation and how they can improve it.

The Exercise

Work with a basic 3-card array reflecting the past, present, and future and use the format below:

1. Select a deck that appeals to you.

2. Shuffle all the cards. Ask the person to reflect on an issue or circumstance.

3. Ask them to do one of the following things:

    - Shuffle the cards
    - Trim the cards
    - Pick three cards.

    Touching the cards so that their attention goes into reading is good for the individual.

4. Thoroughly examine each card. Do not even look at the tarot book!

5. Note all of your emotions, pictures, feelings, responses to the body, etc. Let them flow naturally without caring about being right.

6. Look up the cards in the book to see what it has to say, but if the book does not agree with what you felt about the cards, please don't worry that you're mistaken. It is necessary not to allow the book to set limits on a particular card. The most important aspect of reading is your thoughts and emotions on how the card relates to the person.

Dowsing

Dowsing is a simple and fast way to get responses to questions that have a "yes" or "no" answer. To be proficient in dowsing is to train to ask the right questions. Practice is required! Many individuals use dowsing to find missing objects. This will take as much time as just looking yourself, so the list of questions can be long. Is the missing object in your wardrobe, in your desk, in your den, in your car, in your office, or did it slip out of your wallet?

A more realistic approach to use dowsing is to inquire if a new career is right for you or not. It could be better to have another person quietly ask the questions so that there is little effect on how you treat the instrument by the foreknowledge of the question and your feelings about the response. If you know what the individual is asking, you may be pushing the instrument subconsciously.

Exercise

1. Pick a tool you find attractive.

2. Keep holding it and try to keep the arms balanced. Lean your elbows on your lap or the table.

3. Have the questioner settle on three questions that have answers to “yes” or “no.” For a moment, you could let them keep the tool.

4. Ask for the method to show you a yes answer (allow up to 30 seconds to show a uniform pattern).

5. Ask the tool to give you no answer (again, allow up to 30 seconds to show a regular pattern).
6. Have the questioner ask one by one aloud the first two questions, allowing the method ample time to show a coherent sequence.

7. Register your responses.

8. Make the questioner quietly ask the final question.

9. Check out any other questions if you have extra time.

Scrying

Scrying is a strategy that can target those who are creatively inspired. Long periods of sitting passively and looking at a tool are required. To capture what you see, it is nice to have some kind of method nearby. Perhaps the simplest thing is an audio recording. Scrying can be used to acquire personal insight into your problems.

Exercise

1. Pick a good scrying tool, such as a crystal, a lamp, a mirror, or a water cup.

2. Keep the tool, spend a bit of time with it, and carefully study it.

3. Have your questioner accept an ask or scenario about which they

like advice. For a second, let them keep the tool. Or, take some time debating your question if you are scrying for yourself.

4. Place the instrument so that there are a few items in the room that can impact it.

5. Try to calm your eyes and look at the tool's surface. Seeing just below the surface is useful occasionally. You can check for any surface changes, such as ripples, cloudy patches, mist, etc. They may or may not translate into pictures.

6. Be mindful of any experiences such as ideas, desires, images, impulses, feelings of the body, etc.

7. Unwind. Relax. For certain entities, this may be a more complicated craft.

8. Report any results.

Working with intuitive tools will speed up your intuitive progress, but take a break and try something else if you get overwhelmed or feel too much knowledge to absorb. Please know, there is no hurry, and you can still come back at some time and try the exercises again.

Getting irritated can obstruct the psychic pipeline in every direction, so remain flexible and stick to what you love.

Working with the spirit world, whether you want to be a medium, want to connect and understand what's going on around you, or just connect to your deceased loved ones, the basics need to be covered. In previous chapters we have talked about protecting yourself and ensuring that you are only connecting to people for your higher good. I always say that it takes time to connect to the spirit world, such as your guides and angels, and build a relationship with them. As I said before, it's like dating the dead.

There are many questions asked about whether you can be 100% sure of who you are communicating with in the spirit world. You can, and this involves trusting in the spirit world and in yourself. They will often give you information that can validate themselves, but if you think in simple terms, if thoughts and feelings pop into your head and you don't know why, or if the information is not yours or has no interest to you, it could just be spirit wanting to say hello.

Spirits are not the easiest to work with as they are not slow in communication, and the more they talk, the more information will be given, but it ranges from small things like maybe a favourite food, to what's in the purse or detailed information about their death. They don't always use their names, or their height or date of birth or death. This is information for the living, not the dead.

I remember once being told by a young lady that she couldn't validate that it was her mother, and I hadn't given her full birth name, date of birth and date of death. What I did give was her kids' details, her husband's details, their marriage, the cause of death, what was said surrounding the bedside as she passed, and stories about her parents and grandparents, as well as a baby she had given up for adoption. The lady validates all of this but she said that if I couldn't give the information that she wanted, she couldn't be sure.

As I say a lot, you can't fix stupid. It shows how much some people want, and how closed they are when it comes to actually wanting to receive a message from the other side.

I have had a recent reading myself, where very general information was being shared with me but I could connect it. I trusted this. As I keep repeating, building a connection to the spirit world takes time.

Also, if you can't see them, it doesn't matter. You don't even have to hear them. It's the knowing that is the key to your understanding.

When I work with spirit now I don't often see them. But I sense them and hear so many thoughts in my head, and see images that flow through my mind.

I often compare it to a checkout conveyor belt with lots of information that goes down. I have to pick, talk to spirit and then talk to you. Thank fuck I can multitask.

Sometimes it can feel like a game trying to figure out the direction that spirit want to take and it's always a reminder that I am not in control.

Connecting to your guides or angels is just as simple, but they can be much more temperamental. When I ask one of my guides questions, she just puts her fingers to her lips and tells me to be silent. This pissed me off for such a long time, until I realized that she was doing it because I didn't need to ask questions, I just had to go within and answer them myself.

Common symptoms of spirit entity or taking on energy that is not yours:

- Lack of energy
- Lack of clarity
- Depression
- Mood swings
- Unexplained pain
- Sensitive skin
- Obsessive thoughts
- Concentration issues

Chapter 7

Things That Go Bump in the Night

A haunted place is considered one which is occupied by ghosts. People are usually afraid to go to these places because they are afraid of ghosts. Many people claim that they have seen ghosts with their own eyes, but there is no scientific evidence. Bless the people that like science. While many may claim that a specific place is haunted, sometimes investigators or, to be specific, paranormal investigators find no sign of ghostly activity when they visit such places. So it means that these places are rare, but even though science has not proven ghosts, it can't deny them either.

Regardless of alleged paranormal occurrences, typical hauntings, such as cold spots and creaking or banging noises, can be found in most houses. People are more likely to witness a haunting as they are about to fall asleep, when they wake, or if they are drunk or sleep-deprived.

Carbon monoxide poisoning has been reported as a cause of alleged hauntings. It is more likely that one would be viewed or recorded where there is an anticipation of a preternatural experience.

According to Owen Davies, a paranormal historian, hauntings in the British Isles were traditionally credited to fairies, but hauntings today are commonly synonymous with ghostly or demonic experiences. Various ghosts are known to inhabit vacant houses and places in other communities across the globe. Jinns are said to haunt certain places in Middle Eastern countries, for example. These houses have traditionally been natural locations for ghosts to visit, with bedrooms being the most common rooms to be haunted, as most people died in their homes, whether they were mansions or hovels. After being vacant or derelict, many houses acquired a reputation for being haunted.

The Stereotypes Of Haunted Places

Benjamin Radford's book, *Haunting, Investigating Ghosts: The Scientific Search for Spirits,* is among the most popular paranormal theories worldwide. He claims that there is at least one haunted spot in almost every town. But he also points out that there has not been a single verifiable truth of ghosts having been found, considering over 100 years of research.

In 1 2005 Gallup survey, 38 percent of Americans, 27 percent of Canadians, and 40 percent of Britons shared the idea that houses could be "haunted.". In a 2009 Pew Research Center poll, around 29 percent of Americans thought they had been in contact with someone who had died. And according to data from a Polling Co. survey published in 2020, 40 percent of Canadian women and 25 percent of Canadian men believe in haunted houses.

There is a practice in Japan, related to Buddhism, of building obakeyashiki (ghost houses) in August, when ancient spirits are thought to come. To feel cooler in the humid summer temperatures, people can go to haunted houses to listen to scary stories or look for extravagant decorations and costumes to trigger shivers.

Because of the local cultural myths about ghosts and hauntings, the Shanghai Disneyland Park designers opted against constructing The Haunted Mansion. It would have been deemed a parody of their terror to build the home. The police have created a haunted house in Wuhan, China, to prepare their police force by checking their nerves. A dilapidated house was packed with fake broken heads, bones, skeletons, and a horrific environment of lightning and thunder. The house is also open to the public.

Investigations of a Haunted Place

Investigations of suspected hauntings often lead to clear explanations. In a known haunted house in Somerset, England, in the eighteenth century, by leaping on a beam in an adjacent site that extended through both properties, a child would make the house shake. In 1857, to lend them the ghostly impression of wandering on their own, a 12-year-old girl admitted to wrapping her long hair around things. Tina Resch, a Columbus, Ohio girl who believed that there was ghostly and demonic activity in her home, was photographed tossing a phone while appearing shocked at the unexpected activity of the poltergeist.

In 2003, Ben Radford, with the Scientific Investigation Committee on Ghost Claims, initiated an investigation into a supposedly haunted house in Buffalo, New York. In the article by someone named Tom (real names not used), he said that the owner of the house alleged that at night he felt his foot tapping. According to Tom's description by the owner , "I get a tapping on my foot, not a repeated touch, an attempt-to-wake-you-up tap. After the tapping, if I don't pay close attention to it, then I get a blow." Radford suggests that tapping was probably a case of hypnagogic hallucination (a sensory distortion that happens in the sleep transition). This fairly normal occurrence can quickly lead to misperceptions.

According to Radford, when one person (often a spouse) takes on the symptoms of another, "that can be clarified by advice and what psychologists call Folie à deux." Tom also states that "it will kick the bed, it will strike the side of the bed. I sense my whole body shaking. Then I start to get a good nap; but if I go back to sleep, that's when it happens again." Radford says this was possibly due to disturbed leg syndrome in which a leg jerk rattled the bed in the middle of the night.

Radford believes that the owner's diagnosis of "sleep apnea" is further confirmation of this explanation; restless leg syndrome is probably one of the most frequent apnea symptoms. Tom and Monica have heard ghostly music and voices, sounds that they reported from the top of the stairs, prompting them to fearfully flee their house. Radford performed an experiment where, in the same place, he set the recording system, switched it on, and walked outside with Tom, continuously chatting. Returning to the home, they listened to the tape. Their voices, though muffled, could be distinctly heard.

The pair decided that what they had always heard in their house was outside sounds and not ghost noises. Another test conducted by Ben Radford was to study the theory that ghosts drain batteries in haunted places. To evaluate this theory, Radford bought four sets of similar batteries, packed them in Ziploc bags, signed the bags, and tightly wrapped them in hard tape to avoid tampering. In the reputed haunted Wolfe Manor in Clovis, California, he set half of them in one location and the other half in a different location. Twenty-four hours later, he checked the batteries using a metre and found no battery drainage in either area.

It's common to hear of things moving and shadows being seen. I don't always think that they are bad, as I do think that this is a way spirit shows us that they are around, but I have also heard of things being thrown across rooms and people being hurt. I don't personally consider these to be your spirit family just wanting to say hello.

Sometimes they seem to be spirits that are stuck or want to hurt the people that are in the environment. I do feel that this can be fear based for them, when things are being changed and the spirit does not have any control.

I also suggest that not all homes need clearing and smudging if there is spirit in a home, as not all spirit is bad and needs to be released.

I do believe that there is such a thing as unfinished business from people who have passed, but it's more when they have done their life review and then see everything and all things that they didn't do while they were alive.

Spirit have the most amazing way of continuing to get their message across, and they often repeat things that we need to know and see.

I have watched on television programs about spirits being stuck here or haunting places, and there have been very famous cases, but in my experience there is limited visual evidence. I do, however, believe that it happens.

From what I have heard, the reasons range from the spirit loving the place or home to just wanting to hang out.

So, I wanted to share with you a story of a man that has followed us from home to home. We have named him the smoking man. I don't actually know his name, as he has never shared it. I also don't know why he stays with us, but we first met him in 2011 when we moved to Canada. We came home one day to find this man sitting in our basement. We could smell the smoke; that's all he does.

The man is a kind man, who seems to love us. He sits and smokes and not much else, but whenever we move to a new house, he always follows us. I had thought he was staying at one of our last homes, but after a few days he turned up at the new one. I heard the words "I don't like people smoking pot." Then he took his seat, and 10 years later he is still with us.

I am often asked if spirit stays stuck. I haven't dealt with many, but you do get them. I don't think this man is stuck; I just think he likes it with us.

I have been called to many houses where people get worried that spirits are stuck in their home, and then worried that if we cleanse they will disappear, usually if it's their own family. But I feel that cleansing your space is essential so the energy at home or work is kept much lighter. I once went to a home where the basement was filled with antiques that the husband had purchased from all around the world. The house felt very energetically heavy. There was a lot of spiritual activity, not bad, just a lot of dead people waiting in the basement of their house. I saged the house and cleaned all the items in the basement. There was also a portal in the basement , so I opened a door and let them leave. They were not bad; they just wanted to leave. It reminded me of Noah's ark, with the animals leaving 2x2.

I haven't experienced people stuck as such, but I have dealt with some spirits that are so scared and fearful of crossing into the light because it means that they have to face up to things that they find difficult, or people who they have to see.

I recall a time with a man who had committed suicide in the last few months, who didn't want to leave his children. He went too far and did not intend to pass. He stayed, and refused to go to the light as he didn't want to leave his kids. It took an hour to convince him to go; I had to get his whole spirit family to come and collect him.

This was a beautiful event as there was so much love pouring out from him, but he was scared. The light and the sound is something that I can't explain. It's like singing but not... I saw the hands outspread ready to receive him.

Chapter 8

My Poor Family

This is a chapter that I was looking forward to writing, but also dreading at the same time. Living with me is like living with a nightmare; my partner and my kids have the eye roll of *oh god, oh fuck, can't he just look down and not interact with anyone?* The answer is no. I do feel so sorry for my family because they have been so patient with me saying, "I'll be 5 minutes" or "I'll be an hour." I know it's not fair but it's a drug. Yes, spirit is a drug to me.

I have met many people on the journey who do what I do, many people who want to do what I do, and others that think *hell no.* I would honestly say that a lot of people would struggle being me, because I sometimes feel like I am on a stage in everything I do. I have been questioned by people about why I charge, why I like vacations, how much I spend on them, and asked whether this is ethical. I have been told that I don't work hard enough and don't give enough. I have been called stupid and fake, the latter by people who I actually haven't interacted with or even met.

That does take a toll on my family and friends, because it means that I am constantly checking in with myself, and with what I have or haven't done. I try and explain it to people but only people in the spiritual world get it. I know that at times they struggle with what I do because it's not a 9-5 job and they don't have me for sometimes hours when I am working, but that is also when we are out at restaurants and spirit want to talk.

In a strange way my family and I are in a semi public arena. It's funny because I have to think of practitioners that I will use, including doctors, chiropractors and specialists, as I don't feel comfortable mixing personal and business when it comes to my private life. There is a funny story about when I was having a colonoscopy, and just after I woke from the anesthetic I opened my eyes and started communicating with spirit for the lady that was standing next to me.

My partner is a very laid back person 90% of the time, except when we can't even go to the movies without people asking me questions about spirit and the work I do, or asking me if their mom or dad is ok. The other thing is when spirits are pushing to share a message and it doesn't matter the time of day or where I am.

I am the person who has given messages in the hardware store, the grocery store or even in the street. I will only do this when I am being pushed ... and I mean pushed. The feeling for me is that if I don't do it, I can't move forward. It's hard to explain to people who haven't experienced it, but it does annoy the shit out of people around me.

I have met people in restaurants and then been two hours longer because I have ended up sharing many messages from the spirit world. I was asked by someone whether I was right to do this, and my response was spirit doesn't work on a timer so how could I. It's like when I have been to a reading and at exactly 60 minutes the timer goes off and I am told that the connection is closed. Fuck me, I would love to know how they do it. I do understand boundaries and I have gotten better with those over the years but fuck... My partner has a thing for coughing loudly or rolling the eyes. That's where I must get it from.

There are many days when we sit watching television and spirits like to start talking and giving me messages. It's funny to watch when I am trying to watch television and little old ladies and men, and children line in my mind's eye. You have to picture a post office queue. They impart messages and images, and after a while they start disappearing, leaving me with things to share but no one to share them with. Then it's time to go on social media, post and wait for the responses. This takes hours. I feel good that I have done it, but my partner and family don't agree.

My partner said it's like having to share me with people who at times don't appreciate the effort and heart that I put into my work. I often look at him as the pillar. He is a rock for me emotionally, as he has heard me recount my thoughts and feelings about what has happened. All he does is remind me that I am loved.

I once explained it as if I am having a constant affair with someone that is not here. I am truly sorry to my family for what I put them through. ad It's also the lesson of boundaries that I have, and continue to have to put up. I think I should be able to say no when I am in the grocery store and someone asks for a reading ..... but it's what happens on a weekly basis.

I am also very conscious of how my energy affects my family and friends. As an empath I am constantly drawing others' stuff, so I have to ground and bubble on a daily basis, and sometimes more than once a day. I also say thank god I have a store that I can get incense from as I go through over 100-150 incense sticks a week, cleansing and clearing.

I have been asked whether I read my own family and friends. In most cases the answer is no. It's so hard to give messages to them because the human part of me has to step aside and not let my own feelings and thoughts cloud my messages given.

It's sometimes like mixing business and pleasure. Sometimes what I am hearing goes against what the friend or family wants to hear, so they don't hear it. I have personally found that families are the worst for this. So I stop talking until I am asked.

My wider family to some degree is aware of what I do, but it's not discussed. Some of them don't believe in what I do and are not open to anything, and the others don't fully understand it.

Chapter 9

The Power of Fuck It!

My favourite words seem to be fuck it... it's such a powerful couple of words and affects people in many ways. Some people really don't like the words and they shudder when I utter them, and others know that it's me. Most people say that because I use words like this, it shows how down to earth I am. I also just read something that said intelligent people swear. I like that. I'll stick with it.

I look at these words as me taking control back and owning how I feel. Have you ever thought you need to surrender to the universe to see how life plays out when you don't put your own restrictions on yourself?

What is the worst that could happen? It goes back to the need to control ourselves and our options. I am so guilty of this, but the more I relinquish control, the more I find that doorways open in ways that I didn't know were possible.

I have a belief in life which is simple, and it's a mantra. You can't be what someone else wants you to be, whether that is work, relationships, or personality. You have to be you and live your best life. Just think if you had a life where you had no choice, no decisions, and you always did what others wanted. How would you feel? The answer is simple. Like shit.

To be you, it's a lifetime of saying yes and no to different things and people, but at the end of the day, you have to be happy with your own decisions. I get so fed up when people say that they can't do this or that, or that someone stops them from doing what they want. It is actually a lie, as it's easier not to do the things that you wish.

I remember I started my work life wanting to be an accountant and then moved into different things, but I was always told to be me. I remember coming out and that wasn't easy either, but I couldn't live a lie about who I was. As I write this an ah ha moment came.

How many things that I have in my life today depended on that one decision to come out? Life is short, and we have to do things that we need to do.

The question was asked of me, does it matter what others think of you? To answer this I had to think long and hard. The answer is no. However, the human part of everyone will be affected if people don't like us, but we have to look at the reasons and rationale behind them and that decision. Remember you can't fix stupid. Be the best you can.

Do you really know who you are? I have asked this question to so many people and the answer is always the same. I am a mother, I am a father, I am a daughter, I am this or that when it comes to work, but a lot of people don't know who they really are. They have to think about it. It's crazy that they have to think about who they are but it's so true for many people.

A Simple Exercise

Choose a piece of paper and answer the following questions:

1. What makes you the person you are today?

2. What are the things that you want to do in this life?

3. What are the things that you do in your life that are not helping you?

4. Who stops you from being the person you want to be?

5. What are you going to do about this?

6. Last but not least, are you happy?

The answers will be interesting reading for you. Remember to reflect on truth and honesty when answering them all.

To help you I have answered them as well:

1. What makes you the person you are today?
   Kind, caring, honest, integrity, love travel, love reading, love my job

2. What are the things that you want to do in this life?
   More travel, spend more time writing, helping others without doing it for them. Be my best version of myself.

3. What are the things that you do in your life that are not helping you?
   Boundaries. Boundaries. Boundaries.

4. Who stops you from being the person you want to be?
   Me

5. Last but not least, are you happy?
   I am a work in progress. I am not happy yet, but I am starting to love myself.

To do this makes you think about the areas in which you have work to do. You will see that I answered about me, not my partner or my kids, or my family or friends. If you can't do this, you really can't be there effectively for anyone else. You must be able to love yourself and be happy within yourself in order to be able to help everyone that wants a piece of you.

Making peace with myself is going to be a long journey. But it doesn't have to be all bad. I think as a medium part of my peace is watching others find peace, but as I said to someone the other day, I am learning to feel what people say to me, not just hear them. That is a big thing that many people are going through.

One thing that I do regularly is look at myself in the mirror and see what other people see. This is going to be difficult for some, but it's back to honesty and truth.

One thing that I have realized and had to accept is that you have to love all your incarnations in order to love the present-day one.

Chapter 10

Getting the Voices to Stop

Meditation is an activity in which an individual applies a strategy to develop attention and awareness, and retain a psychologically calm and emotionally comfortable, stable environment, such as concentration or focusing the mind on a particular object, thought, or behaviour.

Meditation is practised in various religious practices. The oldest meditation accounts (dhyana) are found in the Vedas, and meditation plays a prominent role in Hinduism and Buddhism's contemplative repertoire. Asian meditative methods have spread to other communities since the 19th century, in which they have also undergone use in non-spiritual contexts, such as trade and wellbeing.

But there is the main question that arises, and that is why meditation? The answer is meditation can decrease stress, panic, depression, and distress dramatically, and increase calm, vision, self-concept, and health. A study is underway to better understand the health outcomes (psychological, behavioural, and biological) and other meditation fields.

One of the most important reasons people attempt meditation is stress relief. One report stated that meditation lived up to its reputation for minimizing stress. Mental and physical stress usually cause heightened levels of the tension hormone cortisol. All the destructive consequences of stress are caused by this, such as the release of cytokines called inflammatory chemicals.

Such effects can interrupt sleep, encourage anxiety and depression, raise blood pressure, and lead to tiredness and cloudy thought. A meditation form called "mindfulness meditation" decreased the inflammatory response induced by stress in an 8-week trial.

Some types of meditation can contribute to enhanced self-image and a more optimistic perspective on life. One test of medications offered to more than 3,500 people, for example, showed that meditation on mindfulness helped symptoms of depression.

Similarly, a study of 18 reports found that, relative to participants in a test group, people undergoing meditation therapy reported decreased symptoms of depression. Other research showed that, relative to those in a test group, individuals who performed a meditation task reported less suicidal feelings in comparison to those who saw negative images.

Our minds are engaged in a constant internal debate for most of our waking lives, in which the sense and emotional connections of one idea activate the next. We hear a piece of music and, suddenly, we're dreaming about the first time we heard that song with our father or mother, and how that relationship ended because they are not alive now. If we already have emotional distress over the end, those emotions will boil up, and then our mind can turn into criticism, self-pity, or other potential issues.

Our brain creates stories all day long about our jobs, fitness, finances, families, or that strange look the store clerk gave us. We are also not even aware of the internal music that unfolds in our heads, but it is the biggest cause of tension in our lives. Although the mind can construct tales that reinforce life, it has what neuroscientists refer to as a prejudice of sadness, a propensity to pay greater attention to negative experiences than to optimistic ones.

Millions of years ago, the negativity bias emerged as a survival instinct, as our ancestors placed even more time on avoiding future risks than on benefits. It would have used precious attentional energy to avoid savouring a tasty meal or admiring a Paleolithic sunset, leaving our ancient ancestors more liable to be attacked by a predator. A lot of concern was paid to troubles by those who lived to carry on their genes. Their legacy is a mind that is primed to concentrate on traumatic feelings and continues to get trapped in conditioned cognitive habits, returning to emotions of fear, depression, and limitation over and over again.

Meditation is the best weapon we have to fight the bias of the brain's dissatisfaction, relieve chronic tension, encourage optimistic experiences and intentions, and appreciate the peace of consciousness of the present moment.

It has proved challenging to describe meditation as it encompasses various diverse activities in multiple traditions. The terms "meditation" and the expression "meditative practice" are frequently used imprecisely in common usage to describe activities used across many cultures. These can include almost everything that is believed to train the mind's attention or to teach relaxation or compassion.

Meditation may be an old practice, but to establish a sense of peace and inner harmony, it is still practised in communities worldwide. While many various religious teachings are related to the practice, meditation is related to spirituality, and is more about shifting consciousness, finding knowledge, and seeking harmony. These days, meditation is growing in popularity with the greater need to relieve tension in our chaotic schedules and stressful lives. While there is no right or wrong way to meditate, choosing a practice that fits your needs and complements your personality is crucial.

There are nine different types of meditation:

- Mindfulness meditation
- Spiritual meditation
- Focused meditation
- Movement meditation
- Mantra meditation
- Transcendental meditation
- Progressive relaxation
- Loving-kindness meditation
- Visualization meditation

Not all forms of meditation are good or suitable for all. Such activities demand specific abilities and mindsets.

Mindfulness Meditation

Mindfulness meditation comes from Buddhist teachings and is the most common method in meditation in the West.

In mindfulness meditation, you pay attention to your emotions as they move through your brain. You should not control or get irritated with your feelings. You are merely observing any patterns and taking care of them.

This exercise blends consciousness with concentration. While you experience physical stimuli, emotions, or feelings, you may find it useful to concentrate on an entity or your breath. For those who don't have an instructor to direct them, this form of meditation is fine since it can be easily done alone.

Spiritual Meditation

Spiritual meditation is used in ancient religions, such as Hinduism and Daoism, and the Christian faith. When you focus on the silence surrounding you and pursue a deeper link with your God or world, it is close to prayer. To enhance spiritual meditation, essential oils are widely used. You can practise this type of meditation at home or your worship place. For those who excel in solitude and pursue spiritual development, this activity is helpful.

Focused Meditation

Focused meditation involves any of the five senses, using focus. You can focus on something natural, such as your breath, for instance, or you can add on external factors to help concentrate your mind. Try counting mala beads, listening to a gong, or gazing at the flame of a candle. In principle, this technique can be easy but, at first, it may be challenging for beginners to keep their concentration for more than a few minutes. If your mind wanders, you must return to practise and refocus. As the name suggests, this activity is perfect for someone who wants extra attention in their life.

Movement Meditation

While most people think about yoga when referring to movement meditation, roaming in the forests, planting, qigong, and other subtle modes of motion may be part of this activity. It's an effective form of meditation where the action guides you. For individuals who find peace in motion and choose to let their minds drift, movement meditation is great.

Mantra Meditation

In several teachings, including Hindu and Buddhist practices, mantra meditation is prevalent. To clear the mind, this form of meditation uses a repeated tone. It may be a word, phrase, or tone, such as the famous "Om." Whether the mantra is spoken loudly or softly, it does not matter. You'll feel more alert and in tune with your surroundings after repeating the mantra for some time.

This makes it easier for you to experience deeper states of consciousness. Some individuals love mantra meditation because they find it easier to concentrate on a phrase than on their breath. This is indeed a fantastic activity for those who do not like solitude and love repetition.

Transcendental Meditation

A common form of meditation is transcendental meditation. This meditation has been the subject of several experiments in the science world. It is more flexible than mantra meditation, which uses a mantra or sequence of unique words to each practitioner. Transcendental meditation is for those who enjoy the framework of meditation practice and are adamant about sustaining it.

Progressive Relaxation

Progressive relaxation is also regarded as body scan meditation, a technique to decrease discomfort in the body and encourage relaxation. This meditation method also requires steadily contracting and calming one muscle group in the body at a time. In certain situations, it can even allow you to visualize a gentle wave running over your body to help relieve the anxiety. This type of meditation is also used to alleviate tension and clear the mind before bedtime.

Visualization Meditation

Visualization meditation is a practice based on visualizing meaningful scenes or memories to promote relaxation, harmony, and calm. For this process, it is important to vividly imagine the scene and add as much depth as possible, using all five senses. Another method of meditation on visualization requires imaging yourself completing tasks, which are meant to increase concentration and inspiration. Often individuals use visualization meditation to improve their mood, decrease tension levels, and encourage inner harmony.

Loving-Kindness Meditation

This sort of meditation reinforces emotions of love, kindness, and acceptance towards oneself and others. Usually, it means opening the mind to accept love from others and then giving loved ones, relatives, acquaintances, and all living creatures a series of good wishes. This type of meditation is meant to inspire compassion and kindness; it may be suitable for those who experience resentment or frustration.

Starting the Practice of Meditation

Sitting calmly and concentrating on your breath is the best way to start. You can sit for 20 minutes a day in silence, unless you are too busy. You can stay for an hour, then. All this being said, it's best to start and rise from there in brief periods, maybe 5 or 10 minutes.

Pedram Shojai advises, "Sit steadily for 20 minutes every day and do this for 100 days straight.

Pair that with an extra 2 to 5 minutes of meditation to cut ties to chaos throughout the day, and you will eventually feel the advantages."

Meditation and Spiritualism

We humans have relied on divine instructors' teachings for as long as we have been embarking on the spiritual path. Wisdom, compassion, divine strength, and modesty are the hallmarks of a true spiritual leader. Self-styled gurus who toot their horns of "spiritual enlightenment" appear to be mistaken and drive people astray quickly, whether or not their intentions are pure.

The path through meditation toward spiritual consciousness requires patience. Progress is surely not made overnight; promises of a fast fix are, at best, unrealistic. It requires lots of discipline and practice to reach spiritual realization, but the long-term results are unparalleled.

Spiritual Power Through Meditation

Some individuals falsely believe that gaining "superpowers" such as telepathy, the ability to cure oneself and others, awareness of past lives, dreams of the future, levitation, and so on is the point of pursuing spiritual meditation. There is sure to be a snake-oil guru out there who will guarantee them about everything they can think, as long as they accept the job.

The allure of incredible supernatural forces will overwhelm the essential simplicity of the practice of spiritual meditation. Spiritual understanding begins with being truthful and kind, and our determination to being the best human being that we can be.

A powerful urge for beauty and miracles makes the wonder of being alive, and all that goes into making this happen, very difficult to comprehend. What could be more magical and miraculous than the air we breathe, the sunlight we experience, basic acts of love and goodness, interconnectedness, and daily gifts of all kinds? The true fruits of spiritual awakening are benevolent enjoyment of the present moment and an attitude of benevolence toward all living beings.

How to Be Successful in Spiritual Meditation

Getting to know yourself is always the first step. Chances are, like just about anyone else who contributes to self-knowledge, you can focus on features you would like to alter about yourself. The first stage in recognizing yourself and becoming friends with yourself is understanding and embracing who you are, with spiritual meditation. It is an absolute love for ourselves that inevitably contributes to unconditional compassion for others.

If we are prepared to stand completely on our own feet and never give up on ourselves, we will be able to put ourselves in others' positions and never give up on them. Knowing who we are helps us to consider others as they are. Giving up is no longer a choice when we interact with what is sacred in ourselves and others.

Free Yourself from Any Grudges You Have

Forgiving someone who has hurt you or someone you care about can be incredibly challenging. But as the practice of spiritual meditation is developed, you can learn that clinging to grudges brings you nothing but misery, and does nothing to benefit anyone else either. The quicker you forgive, the better your suffering can be relieved, and you can move on. Do not let your path to spiritual consciousness be disrupted by a reluctance to forgive. By practising mindfulness and hoping for others' success, you can teach your mind to let go. It can take time, but the obvious antidote to hanging on to the agony of frustration is letting go.

Focus on Your Spirituality

True spirituality focuses on helping people, but we have to work with ourselves first in order to do this. Looking at our souls with compassion and benevolence, we grow to embrace who we are. We can then apply compassion and altruism to all of this. We see that the more we reflect on others' good as we pursue our spiritual practice, the less we seem to worry about our own needs and grievances. We start to understand that we just want to be happy; all of us are just trying our hardest to escape suffering. We are all the same in this context. You should take good care of people, think about their wellbeing, love them, support them, make new friends, make more smiles. It can sound contrary, but we can see plainly that the more we dedicate energies to others, the happier we get.

Use Mindfulness as Part of Your Spiritual Practice

Many people feel that mindfulness is a tremendous help to exercise their faith, and an ideal way to nourish their souls. In their meditation area or worship place, they find a source of wellbeing, or merely through practising alongside other like-minded persons. And it might contribute to spiritual enlightenment experiences that exceed the mundane, as religious traditions uphold the fundamental spiritual pillars of compassion, openness, and attachment.

On the opposite side, rather than accepting faith, love, etc, some people use their spirituality to hide from reality. You stay open to the relation and blessings of the present moment by integrating mindfulness into your spiritual practice. In the here and there, your religion sustains you, and your mindfulness retains your faith.

Be Open to New Possibilities

Although we are all distinct in many ways, such common desires and experiences bind all living beings. We all look to secure wellbeing and prevent misery, from the smallest bee to the mightiest elephant . Besides, without others, none of them might potentially live. The reality of our interconnectedness can be opened to us through guided spiritual reflection, and help us revitalize our significance. We are just a small but essential part of the bigger picture, a speck of interstellar dust in the cosmos, or like a grain of sand.

We should open our eyes to all the opportunities that this liberation provides us with, rather than being trapped in self-importance. Right now, we should welcome transformation and move on towards a deeper moral consciousness.

Be Authentic

The often-repeated phrase "be yourself" helps you avoid believing that you are anyone or anything that you cannot impress others or cover your vulnerabilities. Unfortunately, many individuals have become so addicted to living lives of make-believe that they have no idea how to be real; that is, to be simply themselves. If the person you are at home is distinctive from who you are at the workplace or with mates, you might want to look at the behaviour more carefully and see whether or not it contributes to your wellbeing and that of others. Being truthful, open, and full of honesty is accepting authenticity.

Precious partners on the road to genuine honesty are the insight and openness fostered by meditation practice. Spiritual meditation will lead to a balanced, rich inner life alongside mindfulness's physical and mental benefits. People are interested in meditation practice and its results: feeling true pleasure and wellbeing.

There Is Spirit In Our Physical Body

We avoid feeling like we are separate when we are linked to our faith through meditation. Meditation allows us the ability to move away from our self, remove ourselves from our life's demands, tension, and responsibilities, and become aligned with a position within ourselves that is never without something we need. Meditation provides the same advantage to everyone, whatever the spiritual activity. It is a means of attachment, to tap into self-love and cultivate compassionate empathy for all.

The greatest advantage of meditation and spirituality is that, as we become more in tune and associated with our divine selves, we become more in tune with who we are and what we are meant to do in this world. Purpose needed? For a spiritual meaning, consider meditation.

Meditation Boosts Your Growth Hormones

In many of today's energy-boosting products, DHEA is a common ingredient, better known for offering an overall feeling of wellbeing. Why not just have some DHEA, then?

For many reasons, DHEA supplementation is not an effective long-term option, including but not limited to having known and unknown side effects (including lowering the normal energy levels), being reliant on the use of these supplements For many, it simply does not work.

Growth hormone (GH) is the primary chemical responsible for decreasing exhaustion and increasing drive to make us larger, healthier, and taller through puberty, and sustain our tissues and organs during adulthood.

Many financially advantaged individuals (including celebrities) expend thousands of dollars a month supplementing this enigmatic hormone! Luckily, through meditation, you can make sure that your body produces this hormone to its best capability.

How Do We Deal with Stress?

As our ancient ancestors spent their daylight hours hunting and collecting, they were certainly physically tired when night arrived. Although it's no new thing to feel drained at the end of a hard workday, we're collectively exhausted for completely different reasons.

And why? We suffer from a kind of psychological epidemic. Not only are our issues self-generated, but we mismanage them before they escalate out of reach. It always goes back to human behaviour.

In essence, we cause our fight-or-flight reaction prematurely, producing a lot of unpleasant chemicals such as the stress hormone, cortisol.

One University of Rutgers doctor discovered that meditation decreased cortisol in the body by a staggering 50 percent. This alone could theoretically double your level of power! In the end, meditation enhances the net effect of all positive stuff, particularly energy, by dramatically upgrading your body's stress response.

Whether it's drinking another cup of coffee or another power drink, to keep going, we prefer to focus on temporary fixes. The concern is that these short-lived blasts of energy lead to an eventual collapse, leaving us as tired or even more depleted than we were before. While physical exercise (bodybuilding, cycling, running, etc.) is a well-proven way to improve energy levels over the long term, meditation works very similarly and (some would contend) superiorly on the brain and body.

For instance, long-distance runners are addicted to their sport because of the endorphins that are produced. These substances, responsible for a sort of marvelous emotional euphoria known as a runner's high, offer a substantial boost of energy. One seminal 1995 study compared the minds of 12 meditators and 11 elite runners who were highly educated. What did they find? Although both classes' blood measurements showed dramatically improved endorphins, meditation had a strong advantage over running (amazingly). It is said that meditation's natural calming level, now proven by scientists, cannot be copied.

Perhaps this is why so many newly minted meditators report that they no longer need their morning coffee, a "must-have" for many people. Meditation sets the groundwork for a relaxed, concentrated, more profound state of mind that stimulants cannot touch. So set aside your energy drink and focus on meditation.

Get Some Sleep

Sleep is necessary in order to begin the day with a fully charged battery. It is possible that your quality of sleep will suffer if you go to bed drooling about your to-do list. The energy levels of tomorrow are closely correlated with the depression and tension of tonight. If only there was a fool-proof way every night of the week to get better sleep. There seems to be meditation.

The mindfulness gained through meditation puts consciousness into the current time, bringing today's activities and the fears of tomorrow to rest.

Meditation effectively shapes the brain into a deep sleeping system by soothing the mind-chatter that stops so many of us from going to sleep and remaining asleep. Many meditation practitioners sleep so well that, with regularity, they can "lucid dream." Without intense (REM), super-restorative, energy-vitalizing stages of sleep, this is unlikely. In comparison, the normal sleep-compound melatonin is increased by meditation, by at least 98 percent!

Extra melatonin makes it easier for meditators to sleep longer, more soundly, and more reliably. These benefits of meditation make the practice versatile.

Meditation Improves Memory and Reduces Age-Related Memory Loss

Improvements in concentration and thought clarity will help keep your mind young. Kirtan Kriya is a breathing technique that incorporates a mantra or chant to organize your mind with your fingers' repeated motion. Studies have found it increases results on neuropsychological assessments in individuals with age-related memory loss.

Also, a study found tentative evidence that different meditation forms can improve concentration, memory, and mental quickness in older participants. Meditation can at least partly boost memory in people with dementia, in addition to combating natural age-related memory loss.

Meditation Helps Against Addictions

By increasing your self-control and understanding of addictive habits, the mental strength you can build through meditation can help you overcome addictions.

Analysis has shown that meditation can help individuals learn to redirect their energy, regulate their thoughts and desires, and improve their knowledge of the triggers underlying them. One research showed that practising transcendental meditation was associated with lower levels of stress, psychiatric pain, alcohol cravings, and alcohol consumption after three months in 60 individuals seeking alcohol use disorder treatment. Meditation will also help you keep food cravings under check.

Meditation Can Alleviate Blood Pressure

By reducing pressure on the heart, meditation can also enhance physical wellbeing. High blood pressure causes the heart to beat faster over time, in order to pump blood. This can contribute to poor functioning of the heart.

Atherosclerosis, or a narrowing of the arteries which may proceed to heart disease and stroke, often leads to elevated blood pressure.

A meta-analysis of 12 trials involving about 1000 participants showed that blood pressure control was improved by meditation. In older volunteers with elevated blood pressure before the study, this was more successful. One analysis found that many forms of meditation created comparable changes in blood pressure.

You Can Do Meditation Anywhere

People practise many different types of meditation, most of which do not require advanced equipment or space. You can mentally work out for only a few minutes a day. If you want to begin meditation, try choosing a type of meditation based on what you want to get out of it if.

Difference Between Yoga and Meditation

For many people, the term yoga means stretching and tying our bodies into impossible knots with a sequence of physical workouts. But only one component of yoga, known as asanas, involves physical postures. For their wellness advantages, and because they help to train the body for meditation, yoga's physical postures are performed. Yoga is a way and philosophy of life, as well as a spiritual meditation method. The term yoga means union between the human self and Eternal Consciousness. In the yoga method, meditation is the most significant activity, and is how this fusion or unification is accomplished. Yoga is thus a system or science that helps a person to improve physically, emotionally, and spiritually, and meditation is the activity that provides the capability to develop it.

Science and Spiritualism

The core principle of spirituality, that Eternal Consciousness is the true truth, is common to most oriental and some occidental types of mysticism. It is not surprising that mystics and thinkers generally accept this concept. In the last century, in the ancient scriptures of Taoism, Buddhism, and yoga, several physicists have pointed out similarities between quantum theory and the spiritual perception of truth.

Albert Einstein, and many of his contemporaries, including Werner Heisenberg, Niels Bohr, Erwin Schrodinger, and Max Planck, referred to a belief in mysticism. When Heisenberg went to India and met Rabindranath Tagore, a Nobel Prize-winning poet, and a wonderful yogi, he was immensely happy to meet someone who didn't believe his thoughts were insane.

Chapter 11

What the Actual Fuck!

The following are questions I am frequently asked:

1. Why do you get so frustrated when people don't get it?

This happens a lot when I say something and they don't hear what I am saying because they want to hear something else. I do have an eye roll for people and, maybe just maybe, the odd swear word comes out of my mouth as spirits are not easy, but they are clear in a sense, and I can't and won't change what they are saying to suit. I also don't understand what my issue is when I say that their dad is here and they say no, and then after a while say that yes, he is dead. It is what it is. Sometimes people will get very defensive about their loved one but they forget it's them telling me about themselves. Love and light!

2. Why do I repeat myself so much in some circumstances?

Sometimes it takes me saying the same thing many times before it clicks into someone's brain.

Frustrating people are supposed to be teaching us to create our own boundaries and not change the level of our own integrity. If you think about people who don't listen, the only person that gets stressed is you, as they are not seeing it or understanding it. They are really not being affected by their own behaviour. The only time they are affected is when the pity party starts and doesn't stop. Spirit is so fluid it teaches us about our own free will and the choices we can make, and it shows us that just because you start your life with some people in it, you don't have to end your life with the same people. People come and go, and new people come. Think about it. How fucking cool that you get to experience all these things and people.

One thing I would always recommend is to give yourself time and space to think about what you are wanting and when you are wanting. This is reality because timing is always the key to life and although you can manifest things, you can't push spirit's timing for all the things that you want.

Other questions I am often asked are:

- Am I allowed to be me?
- Am I allowed to put myself first?
- Am I selfish to put myself first?

You are actually allowed to do and be all of those things and it doesn't make you a bad person. It makes you a person who wants to be the best you can be, and grow without owning others' shit. Ask yourself, *do I like myself when I am with that person?* If the answer is NO, you know what you have to do.

The gift to yourself is learning to let go of unproductive relationships and how they make you feel. If you look across your family, friends and work colleagues, many people can find at least one person that makes you want to be sick or gives you anxiety and whom makes you feel like stepping away from them or their energy. We have all been to places where we don't feel good, even if you are there for a happy event.

It's looking at these things and people and doing something about them. People sometimes think that it has to be dramatic to end a relationship, but it's not and it doesn't have to be. Look within at these things. Perhaps you have to change jobs, so learn to let things go, cut the cord, and find coping techniques. The worst thing you can do for yourself is nothing.

Cord cutting is something I get asked about a lot, and it is simple. There are many ways to do this, but the way I always suggest is to write the person, whether they are living or dead.

1. Get a piece of paper, and begin writing a letter to the person.

2. Write to them about the good, the bad and the ugly.

3. Put everything that you wish that person to know, and always start with the thank yous. You can find one!

4. End the letter by wishing them well and asking to sever the negative connection between you.

5. Read the letter aloud or in your head, and then burn it.

This process doesn't hurt them, but it cuts away what is not serving your highest good. It's both sad and a relief. But you will feel lighter. You may have to redo it when events or triggers come up but it's always for the best of you. As a result of this exercise, you may find distance being created between you, but that's all a part of it.

Chapter 12

A Guide for the Dying and the Living

I was asked to write a guide for the dying, and I thought it was an idea. In reality only the dead know what really happens, but I have been able to see glimpses. I have seen the colours and the images, and felt the amazing feeling of peace. I have also heard the angels sing. Death isn't painful in itself; it's the way you pass that can be painful. Dying is a release of the physical and the start of the work of finding peace. This can be the hardest thing for so many people.

Death is inevitable for everyone, but so many people are scared of it. It's funny because they are actually scared of something they don't know, and that is the problem. The events leading up to death can be painful but death itself is not. I have been shown many times that it's as quick as closing your eyes and then re-opening them. When we die, we all have to go through what I call the Good, Bad and Ugly book, which is a life review to look at our decisions and actions in life, and how we affected other people for the good, or bad.

As there is no time in heaven, this process can take time. There are people still going through this who died many years ago. Time is an earthly thing and although this is a scary prospect for many, it can also be a thought you have in this life. How do you treat people? How do you affect people? Have you had an honest look at yourself?

I know that when my dad passed recently he was met by his mom, his friend, and our family dog. Although I haven't connected to him since he left, I know that they were there.

When someone is dying, sometimes the biggest thing they need is permission to go; that they are ok to leave and that you will be ok. It's a human thing for people to not want someone to leave, or to leave themselves, but I believe that we have to accept the circle of life.

I have seen people asking their family members to stay, even when they have been living such a painful and unhappy existence due to a health or age thing. The family asking for them to stay is a guilt thing. I have also heard of people who are dying, who are having treatment for their family and not for themselves, simply because they don't want to disappoint their family. This is not people who are positive and working on getting better; these are people who are transitioning to the spirit world.

Dealing with death on a daily basis has taught me that no one escapes it, and that the transition will be as easy or difficult as you want to make it. I have been with people as they are passing, I have been on the phone with others as they are watching their loved one pass, and I have also been a support after the loved one passes into heavenly existence. Every journey for the living is different. In dealing with grief associated with death, no one can or should ever judge someone else's journey within it. It's a very personal journey. I do know and understand with my work with the Spirit world that they don't want to living to suffer, be sad, be stuck, forgetting the good times and only remembering the bad times. As people transition to the other side, the people left behind have to in a sense create a new way of living without that person. This is not easy or fun, but it does happen for many. It is sometimes the anger of the person left behind that actually destroys them, and spirit doesn't really want that for you.

Life is a bunch of stepping stones, and once we have walked each stone, opened each door, it's time for us to fly. But please remember that what you haven't learnt in this lifetime, you will come back and learn in the next. You are only in one life of many that you will go through. You will learn about happiness, sadness, joy, the male and female form, and all sorts of relationships. Sometimes we see people being born as old souls, and that's because they have been here before.

I have said before that I don't believe that the dead miss us because they still have us; it's only the living that do the missing. The signs that spirits send are so varied, and can differ from person to person.

These are the general signs:

- Pennies and dimes
- Cardinals
- Smelling of smoke
- Songs
- Footsteps
- Feathers

But there are many more. It is sometimes really funny when I talk about these signs and people say that they don't see any, but then it dawns on them that they have been seeing them all along. I think the biggest issue is overthinking and over-analyzing. The other thing that I often recommend is, before you go to sleep, asking for your loved ones to come into your dreams, but also ask them to help you remember.

There is something that I do with my dad, when he was living with dementia but I could see him in the spirit world. My sign with him was for people to call me Michael, which was his name. It happened on a weekly basis and the apologies I got when people realized that they had called me an incorrect were funny. After he passed, this stopped.

The more lessons you learn, accept and deal with in this life, the more you will have completed.

People have often asked me about whether their loved ones liked their funerals or they did the right thing. The answer I often give is that funerals are for the living and not the dead. Although I have seen and been told many times that the departed come to the funeral, it's really for the living to celebrate that person.

The dead often give messages to the person or persons that are living that are to validate what events have taken place since they passed, and about their life while on the earth plane but you have to remember that in heaven the Spirit don't carry the baggage and burden on their living existence, so it's often in my experience the pureness of that person that is talking to me, and sharing messages. The humour and personality is the same, just they are a soul, it's not the human body that I am talking to.

As I said, I prefer the dead over the living. The energy, peace and joy of the spirit world are amazing. BUT it's just the next step in someone's journey.

Chapter 13

Past Lives

What to Really Make of Them

Many people believe that they were born a long time ago and they died, and then were reborn to different parents, in a different city, and possibly as a different gender as well. There is no scientific logic to prove that you might have lived past lives, but some religions refer to past lives and make it a very interesting topic. People have used different techniques to remember their past lives, mainly hypnosis or deep relaxation. And while some may say that they remember what they were in the past, it is hard to believe them. Chances are they could be saying that only because they were hypnotized.

Regression of Past Life

Regression of past lives is a procedure that uses hypnosis to restore what therapists assume are memories of past lives or incarnations. Medical professionals commonly view the method as discredited and unscientific, and experts usually view allegations of regained memories of past lives as fantasies or illusions, or a form of confabulation. Usually, past life regression is carried out either in search of a mystical experience or in a psychotherapeutic environment. While religious philosophies that include reincarnation typically do not contain the concept of repressed memories of past lives, most proponents loosely subscribe to ideas in reincarnation.

During past life regression, the method involves the participant responding to a sequence of questions while being hypnotized, to identify the events of supposed past lives. A method is similar to the one used in restored memory therapy. Additionally, it frequently misrepresents memory as a faithful recording of past events rather than a compilation of recollections constructed. Hypnosis and suggestive questions can appear to be used to leave the subject especially vulnerable to skewed or false memories. More likely, the root of the memories is cryptomnesia and confabulations that mix the hypnotist's perceptions, information, creativity, and advice or encouragement, rather than remembering a prior life.

Memory experiments reported during the regression of past life have found that they include factual inaccuracies derived from mainstream assumptions about history, contemporary popular culture, or books that speak about historical events. Experiments with past life regression participants show that the two most significant influences about the quality of memories recorded are a belief in reincarnation and advice by the hypnotist.

Studies On Past Life

Studies say that previous lives are possibly fake memories implanted by the hypnotic method's susceptibility. A 1976 study found that 40 percent of hypnotizable participants described new personalities and used different names when recommended to regress beyond their birth. A series of studies performed by Nicholas Spanos explored the essence of past impressions of living in the 1990s. It has been found that accounts of supposed past lives are highly elaborate, with descriptive, detailed descriptions. However, this is not representative of this behavioural method's validity. High hypnotizability was shown by participants who reported memories of past lives, and patients showed that the experimenter's perceptions were most significant in deciding the features of the memories reported.

The degree to which the experimental subjects found the memories to be credible was more strongly linked to the subjects' assumptions about reincarnation and their likelihood of recalling a previous life rather than hypnotizability. The thesis by Spanos brought him to the conclusion that past lives are not memories. Still, rather social constructions focused on patients behaving "as if" they were anyone else, but with major defects that true memories would not be expected. Spanos' subjects used the standards developed by authority figures and knowledge beyond the experiment, such as television, books, life experiences, and their wishes, to construct these memories. In short, it is therefore proposed that previous lives are potentially fake perceptions implanted by the hypnotic technique's vulnerability.

Indications That You Have Had a Past Life

Everywhere in life, we follow reincarnation concepts: the rhythms of time, day and night; the cyclic passage of the sun, the earth, the moon, and the solar system. Every day around us, we still see reincarnation ideals reflected: a plant rises, dies, and releases its seeds. Its roots are burrowing into the soil, beginning to sprout, and new life is reborn.

Every day, reincarnation, or the regeneration of life or energy happens all around us, in numerous ways and forms. Maybe this is why reincarnation is natural to all of us, something that resonates with nature itself, the very essence of existence. Reincarnation and the notion of past lives have persisted for thousands of years, stretching back to the ancient Celtic, Greek, Asian and Indian cultures, also known as metempsychosis and' transmigration. About 51% of the world's population believes in a sort of afterlife these days, with only 7% claiming we are eventually reincarnated.

One of reincarnation's most inherent beliefs is that most of us have led multiple lives before, and even these former lives will be recalled. We prefer to classify these past lives and past selves as parts of ourselves and our egos.

Recurring Dreams

Dreams are the unconscious mind's mirror. While recurrent dreams can also suggest trauma, fear, or difficulties the brain struggles to cope with (unfinished business), repetitive dreams can often represent events from the past life. Many persons appear to have witnessed such occurrences, seen certain individuals, or sometimes gone to certain locations in their dreams that feel very familiar and almost identifiable. One can often have recurring dreams of a castle from the 15th century that one has a distinct sense of knowing very well, but in waking life, he/she has never seen or visited this castle before.

Out Of Place Memories

There are also examples of young children with out of place memories documented, that later prove strangely true in detail. While out of place memories may be attributed to simplistic fantasies, misunderstandings, or contradictions in the capacity to recall, there is growing evidence that out of place memories may show similarities to past lives.

You Have a Powerful Intuition

Intuition is the capacity to align and reach into our deeper wellsprings of primal experience and intuitive awareness of the conscious and unconscious mind. It is said that the more we grow soulfully, the more we are returning to the source (also known as nirvana, eternity, unity) from which our spirits come and from which there resides the mutual unconscious, a body of universal knowledge.

You Are An Empath

Empaths absorb the thoughts and emotional pain of others around them, in some cases literally empathizing or explicitly sensing and witnessing what others do. In certain situations, although posing as an empath and consuming the feelings of others may be seen as a psychological type of evasion to bypass one's difficulties and blame others, in some actual cases, it can be seen as a symbol of a soul that has endured several past reincarnations and has evolved to the point of transcending the human self and its troubles.

Precognition

Precognition, also known as future vision or second vision, is the opportunity to receive information normally not present regarding future events. In visions, physical experiences, and thoughts and dreaming, precognition can be encountered. Although some believe it to be quasi-scientific, precognition is a very real phenomenon for some and may signify soulful energies' maturation.

Retrocognition

Retrocognition is the inverse of the precognition mentioned above, and refers to the capacity to gain knowledge about previous events that are not normally visible. These past events may be in your own life or the far past at any point. Of course, retrocognition, unlike precognition, is not straightforward to prove or validate. Still, this capacity may also indicate soulful reincarnation for those who have witnessed it (and have been able to truly confirm it).

You Feel Older Than Your Age

Some individuals are still "young at heart" even in their later lives, and some individuals only seem to have been born with "aged souls" in the same way. The perception of becoming older than your age is generally related to being reincarnated several times over. This is mirrored in the idea of the "soul age," where there is a definite continuum of soul development, from newborn souls to awoken souls. For example, if you reincarnated on Earth many times, this would be mirrored in your energy age, and you would display several primitive and childlike features in this existence. However, if the soulful energy has reincarnated several times, many matured and wizened attributes will be shown. You could be a seasoned or aged soul if you sound older than your age.

You Have A Great Attraction For Certain Traditions and Cultures

It is said that, for many cultures or periods, experiencing a fantastic, unexplainable attraction is a kind of residue of past existence reminiscent of a certain location, community, or atmosphere that your soul might have encountered in previous lives. For example, you can have an unexplained link with Asian mythology, Celtic artifacts, or the 19th century.

Unwanted Fears

As described in the last point, many assume that memories or events will pass on or leave residues from past lives in our childhood and adulthood. If this is real or is merely a form of dilemma circumvention, many assume that, in the form of unexplainable worries and phobias, we can feel the reminders of past traumas in our own lives. The fear of drowning in water, the fear of specific species of creatures, the fear of certain locations, the fear of specific numbers, colours, objects, and so on can be examples.

You Feel You Don't Belong To Earth

You can see the need to find your 'home' due to the desire to return to the heart (oneness, consciousness, divinity). This desire, like a runner in a long distance marathon who is looking to cross the finish line, is shared by many people. Souls who have reincarnated several times over, in the same way, express this profound desire to eventually complete the loop and return home. It is also followed by chronic feelings of exhaustion and caution for life on earth, and a belief that this earth is not your own.

Déjà Vu

At a specific point in our lives, we've all witnessed déjà vu. It's the odd sense that we have witnessed or lived a moment in time before. Déjà vu always comes unexpectedly and is accompanied by smells, noises, visions, tastes, and other stimuli. While some say that déjà vu is a neurological dissonance, some argue that it represents the possibility of other worlds (i.e., alternate universes). In contrast, even others consider that the perception of past life is insightful.

But these are only signs. There is no proof, no evidence that would prove that there was a past life. Science denies it, while some religions, such as Hinduism, have great faith in it. Hindus believe that humans have seven lives, and their next life depends on their previous life. For example, if someone was good in his previous life, he would be awarded in his next life by being born to a good family. On the contrary, if one person spent his life doing bad deeds, then his next life wouldn't be very promising at all. After living seven lives, one goes to heaven or hell, depending on his deeds.

Past lives have fascinated me for a number of years. I remember as an older child watching a TV program in the UK about famous people having a past life regression within a one hour period, and thinking how impossible but fascinating it was. I remember having glimpses in my life but I just brushed it off. As I say, it is always the timing we are supposed to know. If we push it, it can get pushed back.

I recall a time when I was in New Orleans, walking with my partner, and in a blink, I went back to a time when I was wearing a white linen suit with a hat. I remember looking around at the buildings, and they were so different. I also remember looking across at my partner, who was dressed in "normal" clothing, and I said, "At least I was a good slave owner. I liked to teach them and educate them". I then blinked and I was back. I'm not saying that being any type of slave owner was good or positive, but I said what I said.

That comment has made me think many times over the years, and there are many times, within dreams or while driving, that I feel a connection to a place or people, and there is no reason in this life. That's because they're all past life connections.

Have you ever had that moment in a dream where you have been in another body or sex or time, but you knew it was still you...? That's a past life.

I attended a week-long workshop with Brian Weiss, and it totally changed my life in regard to my thoughts about regression and what it actually meant. The way he teaches is quite amazing, as he talks about his own long journey with it, and so many different experiences. I had several experiences while there, and met some really good people, some of whom I still connect to. I returned there and did the same course with my partner.

I think to date I have completed about 15 of my past lives. The lives I have had are so varied, both male and female, young and old. Each life brought me many challenges, good and bad, but one of the most important things was that money was not important, it was connection. This same lesson has presented itself many times in this incarnation.

I was also taught about speaking my truth and using my gift to help others but not to enable them.

I have completed many regressions for others and it's been an interesting journey, watching people connect current issues in their life and similar patterns that keep appearing, and finding where they started. You can heal these experiences and sever the patterns, if you really want to.

Things to look at would be:

- Similar relationships, whether it be with family and friends
- Fears in this life that are not logical
- A connection to a place when you have no understanding why
- A connection to a person or people whom you have never met

During every regression I do, I always ask to sever anything that no longer serves me in my current incarnation and surround it in a bubble of love and let it float away. This is both relieving and painful at the same time. It's not that I regret things that have happened in past lives, but I am simply releasing them back into the world. It's these things that have helped us learn and brought us to where we are today. I have many more lessons to learn, such as tact and patience. I think this is why I say Fuck so much!

One of my regressions was with a friend, Jodie, in this life. I had an issue with my throat, and food got stuck and no one could figure out why. I did a regression with the intent of finding out, and I was a lady in 1894 in London England, who may have used her body as a way of making money. In the regression, my son in that life, who is my partner in this life, was with me. My throat was slit and I died. After this regression I noticed that, although I haven't fully recovered, this issue is 1000 times better. I also understood my relationship much more. Regressions can help if you want them to.

Regressions don't have to be scary, but they can make people think. They are just snapshots of your past lives. As I have said before, all our past lives make us the who we are today. If we don't allow old patterns and griefs to leave and heal us, we will continue this cycle.

In the many regressions that I have done, I have seen so many beautiful people learn about why they are the way they are, where they started and where their patterns began. It's been both empowering and heart wrenching to hear the stories.

Brian Weiss writes, "A hard life is not a punishment, but rather an opportunity." Even before a regression, some people have pre-conceived ideas as to what it is and what it isn't. I have found that not everyone is open to doing it, even if they want to, as they try too hard. It's not about going to all these lives and seeing what you see in whatever format that is for you, it's about learning why you do the things you do, or behave in the ways you do, and repeat the same cycles. It's about the desire to break that cycle while respecting your past.

Regression or progression is about just seeing the possibilities . I have been a medicine woman, medicine man, seer, grandchild, father, brother, mother and husband. I was on the Titanic, I was a banker in Canada. I have been rich and poor, happy and sad and lonely and embraced. But all of these have been ME. That's the joy of being me!

I want to give thanks to all my past lives for creating me. If I hadn't had even one of those experiences, I would not be here now in this very second. That's life.

Chapter 14

Ego and Entitlement

Why Is Ego Dangerous?

The ego is very dangerous, and is among the worst toxins for our wellbeing.

We can wreck personal relationships, working relationships, and friendships if we allow our ego to take over.

Ego is the belief that the world revolves around us — all the positive stuff that happened was meant for us, all the negative stuff that happened was meant to hurt us. A bloated ego is able to get people to see things differently than they are.

We avoid listening to other's thoughts, and we become dismissive of those around us; we become lost and lonely in our selfish interests. Ego drives people out and locks our minds. The ego intentionally misperceives the light as the source of its suffering. Therefore, ego seeks darkness, hiding, deception, reframing, defences, rationalizations, the pretext of violence, accusing others, blaming society, blaming the world, blaming memories of youth, damning others, suppression, persecution, complaining, resisting, fleeing, etc., as means of escaping and avoiding the sun. By purpose and nature, the self is null, calm, quiet, modest, not understanding, not doing.

Entitlement

Entitlement is one of the most dangerous delusions, and comes with achievement, especially strength. If you're a billionaire, a millionaire, or just a boy or a girl who did a decent job early on, it doesn't matter. If you're not patient, the absolute and complete sense of certainty that brought you here will become a liability. The needs and dreams of a better life for you? The ambition that fueled the effort you made? These begin as earnest drives, but hubris and entitlement are left unchecked.

Entitlement pre-supposes that: This is mine. I won that. Around the same time, entitlement nickels and dimes some when it does not value another individual's time as much as its own. It offers tirades and pronouncements that fatigue the individuals who work with and for us, who have no choice but to go along.

Just before he ruined his own billion-dollar company, Ty Warner, founder of Beanie Babies, overcame one of his staff's careful objections and bragged, "I could put Ty's heart on manure, and they'd purchase it!" He was mistaken. And not only did the business collapse catastrophically, he later narrowly avoided going to prison. With popularity and strength, we start to overestimate our power more often than not. We make judgments then. And our decline starts there.

Control

Entitlement comes hand in hand with the toxic need to effectively manage and regulate. Your ego says, something has to be done my way—even little stuff, even inconsequential things.

Perfectionism may become paralyzing, or a million futile fights waged merely for the sake of exerting their say. It also exhausts individuals whose assistance we require, particularly quiet individuals who do not protest until we have driven them to their breaking point. We're battling with the airport manager, the mobile customer service officer, and the agent investigating our allegation.

For what purpose? In reality, we don't control the atmosphere, we don't control the economy, we don't control other people, and despite that, our actions and resources are a total waste. A wise man or woman must remind themselves frequently of the limitations of their strength and scope.

Paranoia

Richard Nixon's Oval Office tapes offer a harrowing look into a man who has lost his hold not just on what he was constitutionally permitted to do or what his job entailed (serving the people), but on life itself. From supreme faith to fear, he vacillated violently. He dismissed evidence and input that contradicted what he needed to believe. He existed in a bubble in which nothing, not even his conscience, could say no. It led to a tragic and pitiful exit from one of the country's most prominent and influential roles.

After we have attained success, paranoia, another lethal form of ego, says: I can't trust anybody. I am completely by myself and by myself in this. Idiots surround me. It says, it's not enough to concentrate on my career, my responsibilities, myself. I would even orchestrate multiple machinations behind the scenes—to get them before they take me, to take them back for the slights I perceive.

Paranoia produces the persecution it wants to escape in its frenzy to defend itself, leaving the owner a prisoner of his illusions. "Whoever indulges empty fears earns real fears for himself," wrote Seneca the Younger, who experienced destructive hysteria at the highest levels as a Roman statesman.

Believing That Only Your Story Is Great

In 1979, head coach and general manager Bill Walsh led the 49ers from being the worst franchise in football, and maybe professional sports, to a Super Bowl win in just three years. It must have been delusional to dream about taking over a squad so bad at the moment. Instead, he built a philosophy of success and instilled what he called his "performance standard," the attitudes and norms required to succeed.

When you look back on an unexpected or unlikely road to your success, the story is to say: *I knew it all along.* Or even: *I thought this could happen.* It would not be a harmless personal pleasure to embrace the narratives we build looking back. They do not modify the past, and they have the potential to hurt our future.

From that point on, your ego makes you believe that the next inevitable aspect of the story is an achievement in the future—whether it's rooted in work, imagination, determination, or chance. Remain focused on the job at hand, protecting the foundation and achieving progress. Stop indulging your ego in constructing narratives.

What is the Unconscious Ego?

The ego does not realize that it produces and selects all its values, self-perceptions, and characteristics. It does not even realize that there is such a thing as an ego/identity, or that it cannot be altered. It simply believes that the person is the way he or she is, and that life is how he or she perceives it. This is your unconscious ego.

It is massively troublesome. The unconscious ego is almost always unaware of itself. Few unconscious entities have any idea of what their core values and core memories are, nor do they know how they are hanging on to them, behaving in response to them.

This deep misunderstanding is why so many people on the faith journey are surprised by how much healing they have to do. Their arrogance blinds them to the depth and persistence of their egos, which are unaware. Unconsciousness is also a catch because the more unaware someone is, the less likely they are to consider their point of view as the problem. It's not always the case that people will have epiphanies about their journey and their truest self. It's like the ego's weight is collapsing, and the reality is being uncovered. But the weight of unconsciousness falls more often, and only smashes the person further under a mound of self-hatred, misery, and depression.

The Desire To Know Yourself

Letting go of the unconscious ego requires a need to know yourself.

Along the way you begin to build a conscious ego. Whenever it is no longer usable, the aware ego realizes it is made up and can be unmade.

All sorts of enjoyable spiritual encounters may cover them up again; however, they are not gone, thereby generating a new spiritual ego. So the individual is not free, and they don't know themselves, truly, completely.

How To Let Go Your Ego and Return To Heart Again

Face Your Darkness

Letting your ego go means being willing to see yourself as a whole. Many people are delighted to welcome their light and their joy, but not all of us are. There are many old suffering and lost convictions, too, and they appear to be crammed into our inner space's dark corners. Many of the support systems for the unconscious ego are generated by these lost values, memories, pains, and other things. This means that the bulk of who someone believes they are is constructed around this, and once they start playing with this base, their everyday way of thought and living is about to change.

This is where it is going to get serious about letting go of the ego. When someone delves into darkness, many difficult questions come up, and they will go into a time of not understanding who they are or what they desire.

Many people who want to let go of their pride try to get rid of the unpleasant bits so that they can still have pleasurable moments. This is not life, though, but how human beings act. The human being is founded upon a system of happiness and suffering. That's what we all need to deal with. Nevertheless, many people, and some religious teachers, try to say that a life without suffering is possible, and a lot of people plunge headfirst into the argument of pop-a-pill-make-me-feel-better society.

This road leads us to temporary freedom from misery. Suffering is the way the ego makes people upset about situations like a stubbed toe. We must embrace our suffering, and meet face to face with our darkest selves if we are to lead ourselves away from suffering.

Be Resilient When Going Within

Within humans, there are many wonderful things, but all of those are cut off by their egos. Many trapped in self-hate and depression are also overcome by the affection and pleasure that they are deprived of by their self-hating egos. So in the recesses of our hearts, we do find immense elegance squirreled away.

In all of this, though, the crucial question is how much we should yield to our pain. In letting go of the ego, becoming resilient and committed is a continuing step in the road to recovery. When our old unconscious self cries to get free from this, how resilient will we be when it comes to discomfort? How far can we permit upset stomachs that know that our mother kicked us there? How badly can a girlfriend who unexpectedly broke up with us experience the emotional pressure in our chests? How long will the terror of the unknown survive because we don't know what the problem is? These are the types of questions that the Divine puts on the sacred road for all of us. There are exams. How sincere we are, God needs to know. How ready are we to accept life as a whole? And that's part of what being liberated from vanity means.

Embrace The Whole Life

- Be Humble
- Be Compassionate
- Be Giving
- Be Kind
- Be Peaceful
- Be Honest
- Be Open
- Be Loving

This list continues for a bit, too, but they are not the only attributes we feel. We also feel discomfort, but it flies by like moving winds, without the ego to hang on to frustration or fear. Since the implicit ego is no longer there to tell us to be angry that our sports team lost or our friends did not like our outfit, several kinds of rage, anxiety, sorrow, and so forth vanish completely. Beyond the unconscious self, there is a whole universe of fresh and deeper perceptions. But it all comes down to how eager a person is to accept life as a whole. The ego seeks to pick the pieces that it knows are going to serve us well. The spiritual self accepts all.

Ego Defences and Traps

The truth is so easy, but with it, we find so many problems. But why? Because our ego-self knows that its days are minimal and that the divine journey will lead us to an entirely different, unseen universe. The universe is still unknown, of course. It is continually happening before us in unexpected ways, but for the most part, we tend to ignore this reality. By repetition and keeping it as normal as possible for us, we strive to find protection. The acquaintance is recognized, and familiar is always called safe—even though it isn't.

This is no more evident than during a significant spiritual transition, such as a spiritual awakening. It's thrown straight in our faces that we don't know what's going on with us, with life, or how things are going to happen. Certainly, when we turn our focus inward, from the only place where it can be found—in our souls—we can find a sort of "knowing."

But we come up against doubts and beliefs along the way, and a whole slew of ego barriers and traps that aim to drive us away from this easier, deeper reality of life. You have installed these protections, and most of us agree that they can keep us secure.

Predicting Future and Fortune Telling

A lot of people who have an uprising wish to believe that "it will work out all right." Also, most people want to know that the world will turn out all right, regardless of whether they are on the divine road or not. Essentially, you hear several quotations to try to soothe this dilemma in individuals. Quotes such as: "Everything will be good in the end. If it's not good, it's not the end." But what does that mean? It's nonsense. The only ending we all come to eventually is death, and it is very unlikely that the sentence above applies to death. What people seem to say, in truth, is quite the opposite in that we don't want to get to an end.

Our ego-selves want to know that we're not going to be in agony, and a lot of people have a kind of complicated immortality as well as a massive rejection of death.

Yet, the idea is always a hidden aspect of the ego's fortune-telling hand. And if the ego doesn't believe that, with all these metaphysical aspects, you're going to get a healthy and easy answer, then it always decides just to opt-out.

There are also more ways in which the mind seeks to imagine the future. You get caught in this loop if you think you can't do something. Certainly, some facts are more certain than others. Your government will come and look for you if you don't pay your taxes. But that's not the real challenge, and don't let your ego catch you up in this trap. You are caught in this trap anytime you revisit past mistakes and imagine alternate outcomes. Or, those times, when we seek to edit our present realities to better fit our preferred narratives of ourselves.

Understanding this is the way out of this ego trap: "You cannot foresee the future." Indeed, there are patterns that you will notice in life, and the more you see these patterns, the more you will have a sense of where things are heading in your life. Based on the individual's clarity, this is more or less what fortune-telling psychics seek to do. But to be honest, the entirety of the future is still concealed from us, and the kind of decision-making that will keep you stuck all your life is to decide how you continue on your spiritual journey based on whether or not you believe the future will work out happily for you.

Leaping into Impossibility

There are numerous leaps of logic, and they also hide a multitude of conclusions. "If I follow the spiritual path, I won't be able to make money. I won't survive. "If I follow the spiritual path, I can't make money. I'm not going to live."

How have we gotten there? It's like taking a big jump in Kentucky and winding up in China's Tiananmen Square. In earnest. That, at its poorest, is weak logic.

You have to be better at unraveling your biases and decoding your thought processes to find your way out of ego pits like this. It is very instrumental, in general, to tame the brain and bring the horse back in front of the wagon. Until you do so, with these tremendous leaps of reasoning, the ego will keep coming up with ludicrous conclusions, and you will keep yourself immobilized with anxiety.

You have to decide for yourself, what the spiritual direction is to help you tear away the argument, as mentioned above. Most people have no idea, and other people believe they have an idea that is rock solid. Let me stress that making money and helping you is not prohibitive on the spiritual path.

It asks you to be aware of the current moment and connect with it. There would typically be a transitional timeframe if you ever do things you don't enjoy or are not honest. But that doesn't mean the plane is going down either, just because the flight is temporarily chaotic. So, any time you think that life has become impossible, be mindful. These impossibilities are signs that you have taken an immense jump towards an ego hole in thought.

Thinking That You Know What You Want

Too many people feel that they know what they want, but they actually don't have any idea. Let's adjust this to let people know what they should expect from society and their families. You're acquainted with the list. Your list has probably had cash, cars, spouses, pets, homes, work, nice holidays, good clothing, lots of friends, etc. You just don't know why you want these things. The more unaware a person is, the less they even know there's a question to be thought about. My words, with too much ignorance, may have very little impact. It is God's mercy that awakens people from such a deep slumber.

But luckily, you're humble enough to take up the "What do I want?" issue, which is a really strong question because you can't be content with your initial responses. To get to the facts, you typically have to challenge your responses many times over.

And you won't get where the divine journey takes you if you don't. My overall knowledge of spiritual awakening, and my intuitive interpretation of it, brings you where you want to go. This gives you what you desire. Any of you might even have success getting what you felt you wanted, and may be only temporarily experiencing satisfaction before the hollowness pops up.

We have been told to desire very rarely what we want, and if we are really out of touch with our reality, where the spiritual journey takes us may be more than a little shocking. But as we welcome it, we continue to see the joy and affection that we really desire come along in ways that we might never have imagined before. This is why it can be so vital to let go of what you think you want. It allows the Divine room to teach you what matters to you before you are completely honest about this and can more actively engage in the divine plan.

Unawareness Of Spiritual Path

You may help to illuminate your existence or trap yourself within your convictions through your meanings of distinct words and concepts. You're going to be sorely saddened if your intuition is that the divine path will make free you from all human suffering and drama. If you assume that the only way you can be a holy person is to live alone or with a highly chosen spiritual group in an ashram, then you are greatly deluded. If you believe that only a few exceptional individuals can be genuinely spiritual, then you have been lost and undoubtedly lied to.

The more you go down the path, the more effortless it gets, whatever your initial convictions on the spiritual direction. The religious path is clearly what it is. Whatever is here and now is the path for you. You can engage knowingly or out of ignorance, trying to get stuff you believe you like because you don't really know what you are looking for. When every moment and every breath becomes the divine path, you know that you should not be separated from it, and you realize that you are accountable for doing your best to walk it for yourself and those around you.

The ego will no longer deceive you into believing you don't have the time, resources, or anything else to be a spiritual person because you truly realize this. The divine quest is here already; it has always been here.

Getting Out Of These Ego Traps

We come to see ourselves, in so many respects, as our biggest jailer. It's not the administration, our offenders, our parents, our culture, or someone else; it's us. There are wonderful and bad things that people can do to us, but we realize that our emotions, and how to interpret life, can be selected as we mature. But until we grasp the prism we are viewing life through, we can't make those decisions. Typically, doing so means we're going to face a whole bunch of our ego defences and pitfalls that have no reason other than distracting us from the facts.

It is a curious thing that, while it is meant to be serving us instead, our existence should have us so carefully wrapped up.

But it takes commitment and generally a certain amount of time. Bear in mind that you've probably been making this thing for decades—this ego, so what are those years to unmake this monster? And by overshadowing the unconscious self, your eyes open up to a whole new dimension of reality. With that clarity, you can now make deliberate decisions, realize what matters to you, and enjoy the life that you want to live.

Chapter 15

Empaths

What is an Empath?

Empaths are those that have an empathy level that is greater than most. Empathy allows individuals to express experiences, needs, and desires, which may help create exchange relationships.

What is it Like to be an Empath?

Empathy is an emotion, feeling, or state of being that helps one individual interact with another emotionally and cognitively.

It applies to being able to "put oneself in the position of someone else" to better appreciate their thoughts or perceptions. If the connections are personal or technical, this will help establish relationships.

Someone who feels more empathy than the typical person is an empath. In identifying feelings by looking at the face of another person, these individuals are typically more specific. They are often more likely than most people to identify feelings faster and rate certain emotions as more intense.

Signs That Indicate You Are an Empath

People who rate the social reactivity index highly on the empathetic consideration and perspective-taking scale are much more likely to be extremely empathetic.

There are many signs that someone is an empath, and several scientific reasons for these characteristics have been discovered by academics.

Unintentionally mirroring the expressions of another human

Exceptionally empathetic people may unintentionally mimic the movements of other people. MRI scans have demonstrated that there is a synaptic relay system in the brain that helps empaths to emulate others' postures, mannerisms, and facial expressions.

Interestingly, this copying often refers to brief gestures. If an empath notices a needle pricking another human's hand, the brain of the empath may respond as if it were their hand, triggering the same motor and sensory regions.

Mirroring the emotions of another human unwittingly

Like unconsciously mirroring another person's actions, empaths are often more likely to unconsciously mirror the feelings of another person. MRI scans have found that the empath's brain fires off the same neuronal pathways. Simultaneously, if an extremely empathetic person encounters another person who is suffering a variety of feelings, the empath will feel what the other individual is doing.

Feeling the suffering of another human

One small study showed that highly empathetic individuals reported experiencing an electrical shock that researchers gave other individuals. When they were hooked up to a brain imaging system, the researchers gave 16 women an electric shock. When in distress, this system showed which parts of their brains were triggered.

After this, the researchers told the females that their spouses had received an electric shock when in another room. Just as when the researchers surprised them, the woman's brains used identical regions, giving the women some discomfort. This research shows that extremely empathetic people will, to some degree, be able to physically sense the suffering of another human. This analysis was very limited, though, so further research would need to be done by scientists.

Being better and more precise in identifying feelings

People who have higher empathy are usually faster to perceive feelings, especially threatening facial expressions. This faster approach often comes with a more precise evaluation of a human's facial expressions, with extremely empathetic individuals more likely than others to reliably interpret aggressive, happy, or neutral expressions.

Being more inclined to attempt new things

When they see another human enjoying themselves, individuals with strong empathy characteristics are more likely to pursue new things and tackle new scenarios. Conversely, once they see that another person is distressed or displays signs of pain, extremely empathetic people are less inclined to pursue new things or scenarios. I like to say that the best and cheapest thing that you can do for someone is to smile at them. That smile may mean the world to them and in turn, they may smile, even for just a second. You never know when that person needs it.

Being most likely to assist persons in crisis

Other regions of the brain are more likely to "code" pleasant and unpleasant reactions. The brains of empathic people are more likely to be sync to positive reactions, such as empathizing with a money-earning person, and to negative reactions, such as understanding someone in pain. Such brain responses may make it more likely that, for example, a person decides to avoid causing damage to another person.

Being less likely to exhibit hostility

People with increased empathy may have an amygdala (a collection of cells near the base of the brain) that is more sensitive than most to anxiety signals. In reaction to terror, sorrow, and pain, the amygdala responds. Because of their amygdala's reaction, an empathetic individual might be less inclined to be hostile towards a person exhibiting these emotions.

Affection and closeness can overtake you

Empaths can also find it impossible to have constant physical contact within a relationship, which can make intimate relationships hard. You want a lifelong relationship to be linked and established. Yet spending so much time with someone leads to fear, resentment, or concerns about being stuck in the relationship. You may experience an overload of emotions Yet, you consume your partner's wounded emotions and become much more upset as you decide to communicate the desire for time alone. It will be important to set boundaries around communication, time apart and being able to have two separate lives that can be intertwined , whilst having separate likes and dislikes

You've got good instincts

Have you ever noticed why you have a powerful stomach response to items that feel a little off? Maybe you quickly pick up on dishonesty or just know when something appears to be a positive (or bad) idea. This could be the empathic characteristic. Barrie Sueskind, a Los Angeles therapist specializing in relationships, says that empaths appear to be able to pick up on implicit signals that offer insight into others' feelings. "The intuition of an empath often tells them if someone is truthful or not," she says.

You feel relaxed in nature

Spending time in natural environments will help anyone. However, empaths can be much more attracted to nature and remote places, as natural habitats offer a soothing space in which stressful thoughts, smells, and emotions can relax. When hiking in a sunlit forest alone or seeing waves crash against the sea, you might feel totally at ease. It will lift your spirits, soothe overstimulation, and make you relax, just as will a peaceful stroll in a garden or an hour relaxing under trees.

In busy areas, you do not do well

Empaths can absorb positive and negative energies only by being in the company of others, according to Sueskind. This sensitivity can appear magnified in crowded or noisy areas, to the point of being almost overwhelming. Egel agrees, noting that by sensing something more deeply, “empaths can be easily overwhelmed.” Unless you can easily perceive how others feel, you will have a tough time processing the heart-touching “noise” from a crowd, or even a few individuals, over an extended period.

You may feel depressed or physically unwell when you pick up on negative thoughts, motivation, or even physical pain from people around you. As a consequence, on your own or in the company of only a few people at a time, you might be more relaxed.

You’re having a rough time not worrying

Not only does an empath feel for others, they agree with others. Taking on the thoughts of someone too profoundly will make you want something to do with them. “Empaths want to help,” says Sueskind. “But that’s not always possible, which can depress an empath.” You may find it painful to watch others fight, and work on your instinct to help relieve their pain, even though it means enduring it yourself.

People want to tell you their issues

Responsive, empathic persons appear to be wonderful listeners. Whenever they face trouble, your loved ones may feel comforted by your encouragement and reach out to you first. Deeply loving, you will find it impossible to tell people as you reach the point of overwhelming. But finding a balance is crucial.

Unchecked empathy and compassion without limitations will pave the way for “emotion dumps” that can be too hard for you to handle at once. Empaths may also be more vulnerable to toxic habits or coercion. It will leave you oblivious to symptoms of toxicity, in your sincere effort to support people in distress.

You are very sensitive to noises, smells, or stimuli

The heightened awareness of an empath is not just linked to feelings. There are many similarities between empathy and extremely sensitive individuals, and you may find that you're more sensitive to the world around you, too.

This could mean:

- Fragrances and sounds have a greater effect on you.
- You may be more deeply influenced by jarring noise and physical stimuli.
- When reading, you choose to listen to media at low frequencies.
- Sounds can cause an emotional reaction.
- You require time to recover from being overloaded by others.

"Enhanced attention to the suffering of other people can be exhausting, but empaths can quickly become tired," Sueskind says. You might be drained even by an overload of good thoughts, so it's crucial to take the time you need to refresh. You're more likely to feel burnout, which can have a detrimental effect on wellbeing if you can't avoid intense thoughts and rest your senses. Needing time alone doesn't mean you're an introvert. Empaths may be extroverted as well, or slip on the continuum anywhere. Perhaps people will energize you before you hit an overwhelming stage.

To strike the proper balance between sharing time with others and rebuilding their emotional reserves, extroverted empaths may need special precautions.

You don't like confrontations or disputes

You probably fear or deliberately discourage confrontation if you're an empath. Higher empathy will make it easy for others to hurt your feelings. Even offhand statements can cut deeper, and you can take feedback more personally.

More anxiety can also be triggered by arguments and battles when you're not just concerned with your own emotions and answers. You consume the feelings of the people involved, too. Even small disputes will get harder to deal with because you want to fix everyone's hurt but don't know how.

You often feel like you're not fitting in

Despite being strongly attuned to others' emotions, it is difficult for many empaths to connect to others. Others do not understand that you so easily get tired and anxious. You may fail to comprehend the thoughts and emotions you absorb, or sense that you are not "normal." This may cause you to become more private. To feel less out of place, you might stop talking about your sensitivities and expressing your intuitions.

You tend to self-isolate

Isolation can allow empaths to rebound in order to avoid becoming overwhelmed, so it can be healing to block out the world. Yet excessive loneliness can have a mental health toll.

Various forms of isolation exist, and some can provide more vital advantages than others. Where possible, consider spending your time alone outside and meditating in a peaceful park, walking in the rain, taking a scenic trip, or planting. If individuals quickly drain you, consider adding a pet to your life. Empaths will relate more deeply to animals and derive immense warmth from this connection.

You're having a hard time setting limits

In all relations, limits are important. If you're an empath, even though you have no energy left, you can fail to toggle off the desire to feel, and find it difficult to avoid giving. You may assume that limits mean that you don't care about your loved ones, when in fact the absolute reverse is true. Since others' interactions have such an intense effect on empathy, limits are becoming ever more critical. They help you set boundaries around words or actions that can adversely affect you, empowering you to fulfill your own needs.

You see the universe in a special way

Your instincts can be guided by deeper emotional awareness, and you typically pick up on items most people overlook, or draw correlations that are not apparent to someone else. But this expanded link to the planet may have pitfalls as well. Environments that do not have much space for emotional speech, Egel says, will dampen your imagination and sensitivity, leaving you disinterested, disengaged, and unable to flourish.

Often you find it impossible to live with sensory and emotional overload

Empaths can have trouble protecting themselves from taking on the feelings of other people, Sueskind claims.

Good self-care habits and healthy boundaries, particularly around negative emotions and energy, will help insulate you. But when you lack the instruments to handle it, the mental "noise" of the environment will cause serious discomfort.

Suppose you are struggling on your own to handle over-stimulation. In that case, if it affects your quality of life or takes you away from relationships and other personal interests, therapy may help you learn to establish boundaries and find useful alternatives to self-care.

How Does Empathy Connect to Mediumship?

Empathy is connected to mediumship because it provokes spiritual awakening. A messenger empath experiences energy from other realms, such as ghosts and spirits. To better decipher what kind of being is in their world, this empathy operates hand in hand with mediumship.

Differentiating between one's own emotions and others' empathy is a complex term that refers to an individual's cognitive and emotional responses to another's observed interactions. Getting empathy increases the chance of supporting and showing kindness to others. For individuals who obey the golden law, empathy is a building stone in morality; it assists if they can consider themselves in someone else's context.

Everyone has desires. If a person is thirsty, he will drink water to kill his thirst, and he won't feel thirsty because his emotions and sensations tell him that he is not. But for an empath, he has to feel for a person, and he has to go inside the brain of a person to tell about his emotions, which cannot be told straight by just knowing the name of the person. Where his own emotions are concerned, he doesn't have to do anything. They are just spontaneous.

What Happens To Empaths When They Go Around Unprotected

When empaths go out without any protection, they can face a great deal of sarcasm and negative comments. People might even try to attack them, which can cause major injuries. So it is good for an empath to stay protected and follow some strategies. Empaths can protect themselves by following simple strategies.

Self-Protection Strategies For Empaths

If you feel that you are an empath, then you could follow these strategies as a way of helping yourself:

- Ask yourself, "Are these somebody else's emotions or my own?
- If you feel a sudden change in mood or physical state around another person, it's a tip-off that you are consuming someone's energy,especially if you had not been stressed, overly tired , sad or ill before the connection with the person.

It is certainly not yours if you walk on and the pain dissipates! Occasionally, however, the sensation or symptom can be both yours and that of another individual. Feelings are fascinating, especially if they pertain to a hot button problem for you. You are more likely to carry the mental or physical pain that you have not sorted out.

The more issues that allow you to recover, the less able you will be to absorb others' feelings.

To fight negative energy, relax and repeat a mantra

For a few minutes, instantly reflect on your pulse as negativity hits. Inhale and exhale, slowly and deeply, to release the unpleasant force.

Out of the body, breathing circulates negativity.

Holding your breath or breathing shallowly leaves negativity trapped inside you.

When you relax, I seriously recommend that you say this mantra aloud three times in a manner that conveys what you mean: go back to the sender, go back to the sender, go back to the sender. Your voice's strength will force the pain out of your body. The vessel that delivers it back to the world is your breath.

Often, you will specifically breathe radioactive radiation into your lower back from your lumbar spine when repeating this mantra. The lumbar vertebrae spaces are conducive to serving as outlets to extract unhealthy resources. Visualize the pain of the back flowing out of these areas. If it leaves your body and mixes with the giant energy matrix of creation, announce "I release you."

Move away from what worries you

Shift from the alleged source by at least twenty feet. See if you feel any relief. Don't think about people being insulted. Don't wait to change seats in a doctor's office, movie, or other public venues. You don't have to stay and feel awkward if you're alone next to a loud party in a restaurant. Feel free to move to a quieter table. It's all right to lovingly say "No" to those powers. It is an act of self-care to permit yourself to travel. Empaths frequently find themselves in social circumstances that are daunting. Make sure to take breaks to replenish yourself if this happens to you. Then, you will be in a more serene position if you wish to return to the event.

Avoid physical contact

Via the eyes and touch, energy passes. Limit eye contact and touch, like embraces and hand-holding, if you're awkward with others. While embracing a loved one in pain sometimes helps both of you, keep the embrace short if you are worried about taking on their burden. If you were a distance away or it was not possible to be close to them, you can send them love. You have a preference as to the sort of physical interaction in which you take part.

Use water to refresh yourself

To immerse yourself in water is an easy way to dissolve tension and empathic pains. Empaths want to get water! Epsom salt pools, which are soothing, are divine, and even contain magnesium.

You may want to apply a little essential lavender oil to your water. After a long day, it's relaxing. Soaking in natural mineral springs that cleanses all that harms you is the ultimate empathic getaway.

Set boundaries and restrictions

There isn't any way around it. You need to establish boundaries in order to live and succeed. Don't be a doormat if someone drains you. Monitor how much time you're spending listening to the person. 'No' is a total expression! It's all right to tell someone, "I'm sorry, I'm not up for tonight's party," or "Let's talk about it when you're calmer." "I can't tolerate yelling," or "Right now, I need to meditate and be quiet," or "I can't speak more than a few minutes unless you want to discuss solutions." Adjusting contact habits with friends is often a retraining phase, so it will shield you from energy vampires by being diligent about establishing kind but strong boundaries.

Create time alone to regroup

Empaths require time alone to bond with their power. If you have picked up unnecessary momentum, make sure you take some time alone and reflect on yourself. For a couple of minutes or so, leave it still. No sound, flashing lights, telephone calls, letters, emails, internet, TV, or conversations. Often it's important to only feel your energy without anyone else around. You are your own best friend, and this is a way to nurture yourself. It is also easier to detect negativity by reducing external stimuli.

Spend time with nature and 'earthing' exercise

Empaths enjoy nature and are at ease there. Negativity is eliminated by being in a new, clean, green atmosphere or around water. Healing emanates from the universe. Try to lie in a meadow and suck up all of your body's resources. It looks so sublime! Earthing involves going barefoot, sensing the force of the world through your feet. To shed the energy of others, feel the grass between your bare toes, step in the sand or the field. Notice the earth's healing medication coming through your feet to ground you—a lovely feeling.

Take breaks from being available online

You need daily time-outs from software that fills you with too much data. Internet media that stimulates your feelings, including Facebook communities, Instagram and aggressive news feeds, can hinder your ability to fall asleep. Make sure you spend time in nature, meditating, or engage in other off-line hobbies that restore you. Once in a while, full technology can easily do wonders for your sense of wellbeing.

Do You Need To Be an Empath To Become a Medium, and What is the Difference?

Everyone is psychic, and it does not matter what you call it. Whether intuition or clairvoyance sensitivity, we're all born psychic. Every child is born psychic, we come into the world psychic, and then as we start school, we start using the left side of the brain instead of the right. We pull away from our psychic ability.

Everyone has had that feeling of intuition or gut feeling, when they knew something was going to happen. So, everybody is psychic, but there is a difference between mediums and empaths. There's a famous saying that everybody who is medium is an empath but not every empath is a medium. So, to become a medium, you need to be an empath so you can talk to the spirits on the other side.

Why Become an Empath Before Becoming a Medium?

People must learn to feel the pain of others if they are to be a medium. If they can't place themselves in the shoes of others, how will they be able to communicate with ghostly spirits on the other side of the world? A person must first learn to become an empath, and then he or she can become a medium.

Conclusion

I wrote this book with some help from others, both in heaven and here, as I needed to tell a story, my story. It doesn't matter where you started, it matters where you end up, and the choice is yours. You have a power within you that you may not have realized or accepted yet. I have realized and accepted that I am just me, a small person with a big heart in this world. I love what I do.

I love seeing what the possibilities are for someone. When spirits are talking, they see the whole picture; they see the peace and they see what we can't.

My life is not an easy one. There are many reasons for this, but I think one of my choices before I came back in this life was to go through this and swim upstream. It's sometimes really fucked up and messed up to accept that you choose these lessons. I have to work on myself daily as I believe that in doing this and giving a piece of myself to everyone I see, I get depleted. I have felt very lonely, but I know that I am loved. Spirit, although the most wonderful thing to get involved in, can make me feel the opposite, but I know I am a work in progress.

I have no regrets in this life because I did what I did when I needed to. That's the learning that I needed to go through, and I am truly ok with that. In hindsight, if I would have known, I wouldn't have learnt what was being shown, and thus the cycle continues.

Writing this book has made me think, of where I started and where I will end up. I don't know the answer to the latter and that's actually ok. It is what it is today, and then fuck it, but what fun I can have in figuring that out.

It's food for thought for you. Do you actually have to know where you will end up? Maybe instead, work on today.

This book has been a joy to write. It has been hard to sum up my experience with spirit but in writing it, I am hoping that it helps someone. Spirit is what you make it.

My wish for you is to acknowledge the power of you, the power of love and the power that we are all works in progress and that's ok... it's truly ok. I would also hope that you have understood that we are born spiritual. We all used to see, we all used to hear, but age changes us.

My last thought is: You are Enough. You are whom you were meant to be. But it's now your choice to decide what you want to do in life as you can no longer be the victim. Life is whatever you make it. All the bad things have taught us so many things, but don't forget the good things.

A Poem Written for Me

Guidance
In a world where not many understand
He was there to lend his hand
Calm and love beginning to shine
Careful where you wine and dine
Naming lovers and deep dark secrets
Advice like Jesus, damn he knows my weakness
He's like a door, the information he has, intrigues us to want to know more
Guiding souls who are in the dark
His name is Mark
This is my thank you
I was able to find something so pure and that's because of you
Love and light
A world so bright

Frequently Asked Questions

How can I manifest when my head is cluttered?

Manifesting is in reality believing and setting an intention. If you are negative or say that something won't happen, it really won't. Manifesting is free and everyone can do it, but it doesn't mean that everything that you want will happen, as sometimes it's just not meant to be. Also I believe that you can only manifest something for yourself.

Can I tune them (spirit) out?

I choose not to, but although they are always around you, and you know that they are communicating, I don't always feel the need to communicate. I am pretty open to communicating with spirit all the time. This is what irritates my family and friends who I am out with at the time.

When is the best time to communicate with spirit?

Any time works as there is no time in the spirit world, but they tend to be very active between 2-4am in my experience, as it's the thinnest veil between dimensions. I have had spirit in the washroom with me just talking away.

Why am I so blunt?

Because I am. I believe that there is no point in being all angelic and making it out that life is a bed of roses for everyone. It's about the integrity of my work with spirit. I won't ever predict death for someone as I believe it's not my business or theirs to be told, but I have talked about most other things people.

How old was I when I first connected to spirit?

I was 7, but I didn't even understand it or what it meant. It was much later that I started this work with them. I have always seen things but I used to brush them off when I was 11, and then when I was 17, spirit changed me. Spirit showed me things that I needed to see, and once opened you can't go back in the closet. The work I do with spirit can be amazing, but it all comes down to the person receiving the message.

What if the spirit doesn't speak English?

English is the only language I speak , so I only hear spirits in English. In humour I equate it to google translate in my head.

Why do some spirits step forward and others don't?

I believe that it's always the right spirits that step forward when you most need them. It's like being in a school playground and hearing different people trying to talk. It doesn't mean that they are not around; it's who I am hearing. I know that this disappoints some people, but I don't have control. When I tell people this, some feel it should be like a dial up service but it's not. I also like to remind people that there are only so many people I can have in my head at the same time.

What if I don't want to do any more learning in this lifetime?

We are all here with free will, but I do believe that all lessons are needed to be learnt. If they are not we will have to repeat them in different lives. I look at it as coping strategies in this life, and what is the true lesson for what we are going through.

What happens to me when I start connecting to the spirit world?

I feel like energy is flowing through me, and that the words or images that are formulating within me are not mine. I hear thoughts that, over time, I have just accepted as being spirit. It's a whole trust exercise. I do believe that we are all born with this, but it's adults that change children's thinking. I can feel the energy that is flowing through me and when they leave, I feel it too, which is why I get so tired.

Are spirits the same as they were on earth?

The short answer is yes, but they have had to work through the physical issues so they are lighter. At times they say sorry, and other times they just acknowledge their wrongdoings, but they come through exactly with the same personality. Sometimes this is both shocking and upsetting to the person that I am working with, as they expect something different or they are not actually prepared for that person to come through due to the issues in this life. I have had an instance of a little old Italian lady throwing holy water at me from the spirit world. It was both funny and also alarming, but the family I was working with laughed because it was what she would do.

Have I ever had a bad reaction from the person I am working with?

Yes indeed, and sometimes it has been so fucked because they are shouting at me about who is talking from the spirit world. In most cases it's an issue of the living not wanting to hear what is being told as it's work that they have to do and don't want or are not ready to do. I don't do well with pity parties. I believe that we are all able to make choices in our lives, and ownership and responsibility for this is essential for learning. I sometimes think that some people have their own narrative, and that is all they can cope with.

My Spirit Top 5

A lady asked me to speak to people in heaven that she didn't even know or had ever met, but wanted to ask if they would have liked her. I got the person in spirit but they made it clear that they didn't know her. The lady wasn't even embarrassed.

A man came and wouldn't believe anything about what I was saying, and then his dog came. We spent an hour talking about his dog with him sobbing... truly the dog made him a believer.

A man came to me a few hours before he passed with cancer to thank me for everything that I had done to help him and his family with his journey. This happened at 1am and he died at 7am. He had woken up another person at the same time to say goodbye.

My grandfather stopped me from ending my life. He came and reminded me that I had so much to do to help others. He is someone who passed when I was 2, but he has helped me so many times.

I have seen so many affairs, unusual living arrangements, really funny dead people, breasts and all sorts of bits of men and women. I remember a young man once being shown a room of breasts. His deceased friend thought I needed to learn, lol.

What Clients Have Said

"From that moment, even before our reading, I knew Mark was blessed with a beautiful gift."

"Mark was accurate in everything he told us. Mind blowing."

"He asked me to ask her if he could call her. I called her, told her about Mark and what he had said about her son, and asked if he could contact her. She agreed, and Mark called her in England. He went above and beyond to help her, with no monetary gain. What he said to her completely changed her. He gave her peace and insight she had not had before. We will all be forever grateful for that."

"Mark, you have made our lives so different just by us learning about Spirit. When our son Taylor got his angel wings we were so sad and very depressed, unsure of where he was or who was looking after him. Because our son was medically fragile, he was dependent on a nurse to care for him. We met you three months after Taylor got his angel wings, and you made a huge impact on our lives and still do. You answered so many questions for us, that we have become grounded, and we aren't worried about where Taylor is anymore."

"Spirit has changed our lives; we are more open to Spirit and what can be done."

"To say that Mark transformed my life would be an understatement. Mark, like a gatekeeper at the pothole of my realms, delivers key messages to me that are guided by my spirits. Spirits that

I've never met physically in this life but have heard about from family, proving that the string of energy, the bright Mercury string linking us to all our lives, is "Alive" and omnipresent; linking us to crucial information that, when willing, can guide us to our true self. Mark is a remarkable man. His messages have touched me deeper than anyone will ever know, healing parts of me that needed to be healed. I can't recommend him enough."

"My experience with Mark was "jaw-dropping," amazing, and inspiring. He provided information that was so spot on that I knew it was my father. He had this type of humour and Mark nailed it. There were many tears through the session but lots of laughter too, which was my dad. He was always laughing. Mark delivers his messages with compassion and love."

"Wow! I really don't know where to begin, other than saying that if you or your family members would like to get that extra moment to spend with your loved one, Mark is the guy that will definitely make it happen."

"With the loss of my baby I did not get the chance to spend time with her. But Mark was able to help me with her signs."

"Mark's reading brought the mother I had just lost close to me again. His words were so accurate that it felt like I had been visiting with her all morning. I missed her so deeply and his reading was such a blessing."

Manufactured by Amazon.ca
Bolton, ON

20627559R00107